PRAISE FOR *BEYOND MEDITATION*

"Meditation is not a one-size-fits-all kind of thing and as a beginner it can be overwhelming trying to figure it out. Kerry and Mira have given us awesome examples of how to get started and how not to get caught in perfectionism. This is a wonderful workbook full of love, kindness and wisdom. Thank you both!"

> — *Suzanne Alft is President & Owner of Transformation Enzyme Corporation and an advocate for holistic and integrative health care*

"Mira and Kerry have done a fantastic job with *Beyond Meditation*. I know how important stress reduction and mindfulness is for myself and in my practice and I see the greatest impact with my clients who take the time to apply these techniques. This book gives a fantastic overview of different methods, mediations and exercises to help the reader on their health journey and shows them how to incorporate into their daily routines. I have learned so much from this book myself and it is now a highly recommended all-in-one resource for all of my clients, friends and family. Cheers ladies!"

> — *Coleen Walsh, MNT, "The Methyl Queen" is a holistic and functional nutritionist specializing in MTHFR and Methylation education, practitioner mentorship and one on one client consultations*

"For over 10 years I've practiced poi and staff fire dancing as a form of mindfulness. The ability to use movement to feel present in the moment and grounded is a wonderful tool for calming your mind. In *Beyond Meditation* Mira and Kerry offer a wonderful book of mindfulness practices for the every day person based on real every day experience. I love how this book teaches a variety of mindfulness practices beyond meditation such as movement and doodling."

> — *Julie Matthews is a Certified Nutrition Consultant specializing in autism spectrum disorders and BioIndividual Nutrition®, and is the author of the award winning book, **Nourishing Hope for Autism***

"I loved this book. I recommend meditation to all of my Kick Start clients. For many meditation can seem difficult but this book makes it so clear and achievable. Beyond Meditation is something I will definitely recommend to my audience. You will love all of the insightful advice and practical application all written in a user friendly modern way. It's brilliant. Thank you ladies."

— *Rachel Holmes* *is a UK-based Women's Fitness & Health Expert and Founder of the Kick Start Health & Fitness Franchise System*

"Through kind introspection and mind-fullness *Beyond Meditation* takes you on a simple journey towards what most believe to be a very complex practice. It shares the author's experiences and challenges with meditation and also illustrates how these challenges were overcome. It provides a road map for the novice, clearly defining and clarifying how to find your place to start. It also serves a great reminder for those familiar with meditation allowing for new thoughts and an expansion of experiences and results. Learn how to be responsive, in the moment and how to create a greater health within your mind and body all while nourishing your soul."

— *Trey Looney, Founder Halest Health Solutions and long time seeker of health*

"*Beyond Meditation* is a delight! Open, accessible, unifying, inviting, practical, heartfelt. A gift for those who need a road map to find their way home to peace, love and their own essence."

— *Dr. Ed Bauman, Founder and President of Bauman College:Holistic Nutrition + Culinary Arts*

Beyond Meditation
MAKING MINDFULNESS
ACCESSIBLE FOR EVERYONE

by Mira Dessy, BFA, NE, BCHHP
and
Kerry McClure, BS, RYT, NC, BCHN®

foreword by Ajayan Borys

Permission requests, speaking arrangements, and wholesale inquiries may be addressed to Versadia Press, PO Box 1181 Willis TX 77378
www.VersadiaPress.com

Printed in the United States of America 1st printing – July 2017
ISBN: 978-0-9889357-1-6
EDITOR: DONNA MOSHER, SEGUE COMMUNICATIONS
Back Cover Photo Credit In Her Image Photography

Author Contact Information
Mira Dessy www.TheIngredientGuru.com
Kerry McClure www.KerryMcClure.com

DISCLAIMER

The authors of this book are not doctors. The information in this book should not be considered medical advice and is not intended to treat, diagnose, prevent or cure any conditions, physical or otherwise. If you require medical advice or attention, please consult a physician or other health professional. Information provided in this book has not been reviewed or approved by any federal, state, or local agency or healthcare group. Opinions expressed are solely those of the authors and do not represent any particular individual or professional group.

CONTENTS

FOREWORD

Today there is an unprecedented surge of interest in meditation in the West. Hardly a day passes without another study on the benefits of meditation being published. Terms like "mindfulness" and "mantra" have become part of our daily lexicon. And there seem to be thousands of approaches to meditation. If you don't already have a practice, where do you start? How do you navigate such a plethora of teachings and techniques? In this little book, Kerry and Mira have generously shared their experiences and the experiences of others to provide insight and direction, to begin to make sense of an overwhelming amount of information related to meditation.

It is hardly an exaggeration to say that meditation has been my life for the past 46 years. What inexorable force drew me toward my core? I relate my experience later in this book, so I won't go into that here, but one thing I will add to provide some insight into meditation is a phrase from the Shiva Sutras (the primary text of a traditional school of mysticism known as Kashmir Shaivism):

The stations and stages of yoga constitute a fascinating wonder.

Note that here, "yoga" refers to union, such as that experienced during meditation, and not the physical poses you typically experience in a yoga class.

Wonder is what meditation is about. It is a wonder to experience the vastness of space within your consciousness, to feel the blissful light of awareness bathing every cell in your body, to experience waves of love and compassion, and more. At every stage of practice, you are opening to more and more wonder. There are a hundred billion neurons in your brain and ten thousand times as many connections. The result is human awareness and all we experience in this life—

all the thoughts, feelings, and perceptions. Meditation is this human awareness turning back upon itself, to know itself. Meditation is exploring the basis of all human experience, awareness itself, unbounded and pure. What could be more remarkable, mysterious, and wonderful? This is the inmost essence of who we are.

I mention this because many labor under the impression that meditation requires, first and foremost, great discipline. In my experience, nothing could be further from the truth. Does it require discipline to peer into a clear night's sky and enjoy the myriad stars and galaxies? Neither does it require discipline to explore the inner space of consciousness. When you have wonder, discipline follows naturally and effortlessly. Indeed, proper meditation hardly requires discipline at all, though it may appear so to others looking on. Once you get the hang of meditation, each sitting is as delicious as a dish of your favorite ice cream. Eating your favorite dessert hardly requires discipline!

That said, I would like to offer some caution. Meditation is a subtle art. Even one misunderstanding or misplaced attitude (for instance, if you have the idea you shouldn't have thoughts when you meditate), will undermine the innocence of your experience. Without innocence, wonder won't happen; frustration will. As Christ said, you must be as innocent as a child to enter into the kingdom, and the kingdom of heaven is within. For this reason, it is essential to receive proper instruction when beginning meditation. This will likely save you immense time and struggle and years of frustration.

How can you tell if you're receiving proper instruction? Proper instruction will set you on a path of effortless meditation (for effort agitates the mind and keeps it at a superficial level). A wise teacher will never pit you against your own mind; rather, he or she will help you work with the nature of your mind, and so your experience will be characterized by ease. That is the key to successful meditation.

As you progress in your path, you will find yourself going deeper, your experiences becoming clearer, and the bliss of meditation becoming more and more tangible. You will feel these effects seeping into your active daily life as well. This is how it works; growth is real but gradual. Don't expect mystical union your first sitting.

You *can* expect deep relaxation (perhaps the deepest relaxation you have ever felt) in even your first sitting and an experience that is pleasant and surprisingly easy. You can also expect to emerge feeling rested, relaxed, and more peaceful. Perhaps more alert and buoyant as well.

By meditating daily, you will soon find your meditations changing. They will be filled with light, wholeness, and tangible bliss. At this stage, you may wish to explore other techniques that take you deeper and intensify your meditations. Every major tradition of meditation entails levels of instruction that take you ever deeper. There is an inner universe to explore. Don't stop when you reach the edge of the solar system—unless relaxation is all you're after. There is so much more to who you are. As the great mystics have proclaimed, You are *That*, the unknowable Source of all.

Ultimately, that is the gift of meditation: it reveals who we are, in our essence, and that essence is inextricably related to the Source of our existence. As we open to that Source, we gain the gifts of Spirit, all the practical benefits of meditation, from greater mental clarity and creativity, to inner peace and joy, to improved health. And all that is required is to sit, daily. Enjoy!

> *– Ajayan Borys*
> *Issaquah, WA, November 2016*

In the hustle and bustle of life,
stop a moment and take in the view

WHY MEDITATE?

We're all too busy. No matter where you work, the word of the century seems to be *productivity*. How can companies increase productivity? How can they get more for less? "Productivity" really means staying busy, implying that the busier we are, the more value we provide. Who doesn't think: "If I can just be a little more productive, everything will be better"? The push has become relentless. As if driving oneself to exhaustion will somehow make everything perfect. But the compulsion for productivity leaves no time to take a break, to rest, to restore.

Modern life has become so overwhelming and overstimulating that we are experiencing an epidemic of stress and depletion. We, Mira and Kerry, are in the business of helping people live healthier, happier lives. So we are qualified to call this what it is: an unhealthy epidemic. We wrote this book to help our clients – and you – find a way to sidestep this epidemic. We want to offer a respite of calm that, from a small investment of just minutes a day, will restore balance in your mind, your relationships, your work, and your health.

Our recommendation is meditation.

Surprised? Of course you aren't. Meditation has become a trend, a mantra, if you will, in the mainstream and alternative media. You can hardly go a day without seeing stories and social media praising the value of meditation, and it is with good reason. But if you are like the people we work with, learning to meditate may be just one more thing you need to add to your busy day – and who has time anyway?

We get that. And that is why we have written this book. We say you don't have to meditate while sitting in lotus position with your eyes closed chanting *Om* for an hour every day. We will share a range of meditation opportunities and suggest easy ways for you to work it into a busy day. That is how important – and valuable – meditation can be.

Perhaps you remember the cartoon of a man talking to his friend, saying, "I've hooked the VCR up to the microwave oven so we can fast forward our TV dinners." Sure, it's funny, but sadly, it is also true. Nothing is fast enough. We receive oddly mixed messages about seeking life balance, being more productive, finding time for personal development, do more, buy more, hurry up. All of which leaves us feeling overwhelmed and unsatisfied. Modern culture has sucked us into hurry-up-instant-gratification-faster-faster mode.

We believe that no one wants to live this way. The messages that surround us encourage us to do so. For how many years have you noticed that Christmas decorations appear in the stores just after Labor Day? We still have Daylight Saving Time, and yet they're pushing holiday lights and glitz. You may complain to yourself, or to friends and family. But it doesn't change. Rather, it gets worse and more exhausting.

The more we try to do, the faster we go, the more exhausted we become and the less we can deal with everyday stressors. Sadly, this also leaves us less able to enjoy those precious moments that come into our lives. We've blunted our ability to be mindful of the joys that surround us each day.

Combining agitation, hurry, and worry makes a perfect storm for dysfunction and ill health. A high-stress lifestyle drains our adrenals, increases our cortisol levels, increases our blood pressure and makes us fat. When we take time for mindfulness and to slow down the pace of life, even if just for a little bit, we change how we feel. We disconnect from that stress and pressure, and physically our body produces more nitric oxide, which helps our blood pressure drop. Additionally our heart rate slows, our hormone levels change (for the better). There are even studies that show a positive correlation between meditation and improved immune system response.

Studies show that taking time for daily meditation improves concentration and memory retention, which can increase productivity. A meditation practice also develops self-awareness, allowing us to detach mindfully from situations, especially emotional ones, that can be overwhelming, and in some cases, destructive to our relationships or our sense of self. That self-awareness further encourages us and leads us to a deeper commitment to self-care. If we're taking the time to be more mindful, we create the mental and emotional space to see what else we might do that would be supportive: perhaps it's quitting smoking, or changing our diet, or deepening the connection with our loved ones. All of those things become a blur when we're moving as fast as we can. Slowing down just a little bit brings clarity and focus, which allows us to make changes.

Countless studies show that meditation increases happiness. The emotional benefits of meditation can be powerful: less depression, reduced anxiety, and an improved sense of well-being. Research shows still more benefit: decreased impulsivity, a reduction in worry and fear, and increased self-esteem, mood, and optimism.

Memory strength and focus go up with meditation as does creative thinking and problem solving. One study even showed that people who took a break from a complex task had an increased ability to solve problems, in some cases by as much as forty percent. Many of the world's great thinkers such as Albert Einstein, Thomas Edison credit "daydreaming" as being a significant part of their success. In effect, disconnecting and allowing their minds to wander engaged them in a mindfulness practice that enabled them to be more effective and more creative.

Are you inspired to discover all the benefits of a meditation practice? Below we discuss a few of the more common forms of meditation. We invite you to explore several different forms to see which modality services you best. Any form of meditation that appeals to you and suits your lifestyle can be beneficial to your mind, body, and spirit. You may find you start with one style and later begin to practice another style. Like anything you learn, it's a journey of discovery and seeing what works best for your individual temperament and lifestyle demands.

Glance into the past,
honor your lessons, and move forward

Glance into the future and let it be
Come into the present and live

DISCOVER MEDITATION

"It's never too late to do nothing"
– Zen saying

Someone has said that when you say you meditate, it's like saying you play sports. The question arises: So which sport do you play?

Similarly, there are many different styles and techniques in which to meditate. This book is by no means intended to be a technical or scientific account of meditation, nor is it a comprehensive guide to the many different techniques, styles, lineages, forms, and interpretations of meditation that exist. This work is considered more a sharing of our experience of meditation and provides a general, high-level overview of some of the more popular forms of meditation. Our goal is to give you, the reader, an "accessible" approach to meditation and to pique your interest in deepening your understanding and study of meditation.

This book provides a brief exploration of a few meditation techniques and a workbook for learning about and practicing common forms of meditation. It also shares information about the benefits gained from a regular meditation practice. We would humbly suggest that there is no one best way or form to practice meditation. The best one is the one that provides you with a sustainable and consistent practice. This book creates a fun environment where you can try a few different forms of meditation and see which one(s) resonate with you. We hope you enjoy the journey.

Eight percent of U.S. adults (18 million) used meditation, according to the National Health Interview Survey (NHIS) conducted by the National Center for Health Statistics (NCHS), part of the Centers for Disease Control and

Prevention. And according to the National Center for Complementary and Integrative Health (NCCIH), "Many studies have investigated meditation for different conditions, and there's evidence that it may reduce blood pressure as well as symptoms of irritable bowel syndrome and flare-ups in people who have ulcerative colitis. It may ease symptoms of anxiety and depression and may help people with insomnia." Other noted benefits of meditation may include stress relief, anger management, improved awareness and concentration, and improved cognitive skills.

Many meditation techniques use the breath as a form of concentration, as a way to tether the mind and keep it from running amok. Some use mantras, while others also include visualization and sound. One could make the observation that the way we live our lives moment-to-moment is a form of meditation that results in our current reality. Meditation, as practiced in its many forms, is trying to bring further consciousness to this process, to affect an outcome that is more aligned to enabling our highest potential. We each have the opportunity in each situation to pause for a moment and make a choice that responds to the situation rather than reacting to it. This is a form of mindfulness meditation.

As you explore the different forms of meditation listed below, please note that there are examples and guidelines in the workbook section at the end of this book.

Life is a journey of many steps
Meditate anyway

MINDFULNESS

Mindfulness meditation is a Western interpretation of the many styles and techniques that have been taught in various philosophical and traditional meditation venues for thousands of years. It can be defined as being fully in the moment. It offers a sense of awareness and presence by paying attention to the sensations of the breath and physicality of your body and observing your thoughts in your mind without judgment. Mindfulness brings our awareness to the present moment so that we can observe our interpretation and action of the environment we are in. If we can accept how "things are in this moment" without judgment or expectations, then we are better able to respond to the situation rather than react to it.

Jon Kabat-Zinn has drawn from the Buddhist meditation techniques as well as science, medicine, and psychology and created a form of mindfulness meditation called the Mindfulness-Based Stress Reduction (MBSR) program. Mainstream health and wellness practitioners have widely accepted his program, perhaps because studies show the benefits to our bodies and our minds. MBSR programs demonstrate positive changes in the brain, lower stress, reduced depression, and improved memory and attention skills. The list goes on, but as you can see there is a benefit to choosing a meditation technique, or group of techniques, to support a practice of "being in the moment" or "being present."

The purpose of any meditation practice is to raise our awareness and knowledge through observation and acceptance. This can take many forms. We are going to present and consider a few of them here. We shall categorize them by:

- *Mantra*
- *Visualization*
- *Movement*
- *Breath*

MANTRA MEDITATION

A mantra provides a focal point for the period of the meditation and can be something as simple as a repetitive saying to yourself. The use of a word or phrase as a point of concentration enables the meditator to have something to anchor the experience. This gives the mind something to return to, as it tends to wander with varying thoughts. Primordial sounds such as the universal OM (Aum), chants, melodic repetitions, and resonating vibrations are often used in mantra meditation.

VISUALIZATION

Meditation using visualization has been used in many of the styles and techniques. It can be as simple as seeing your body relaxing as you breathe in and out. It might take the form in a sitting meditation of seeing yourself in a special place (ocean, forest, stream, desert, mountaintop, or any other environment) that you use to raise your vibration. It might take the form of a guided meditation suggesting specific scenes to enhance the technique being practiced. You might be active and alert and using an object or objects to enable your concentration (sometimes quietly sitting and watching a fire, or observing a statue, or on a walk observing all the flowers in bloom and concentrating on how that enhances all life, then letting what arises guide us in our life).

Chakra meditations are often used to enhance the energy centers in the body. In the chakra system, there are seven energy centers, with associated colors, sounds, and purpose. Getting a flow of energy through all of these centers enhances health according to Eastern medicine. Sound and color visualization techniques are often used when practicing chakra meditation. Studies have shown that this improves the balancing of emotions. Yoga is often practiced with concentration of the chakra energy centers.

MOVING MEDITATION

This is movement with a mindful purpose. On high-energy days this can be a great alternative to sitting meditation. It is a physical activity done with intent to enable higher function and balance. Examples include yoga, tai chi, and qi gong. Walking in a meditative state to enhance the "now" is becoming more popular. Observing what is currently surrounding you and letting that permeate your senses has a calming and positive effect. Many use the visualization techniques noted above in conjunction with a movement meditation. And yes, with the right mindset you can even make doing the dishes into a meditative exercise!

CONSCIOUS BREATH MEDITATION

Here breath is a point of concentration. Simply observing the breath enables us to realize how busy our minds are as we experience them jumping from one thing or thought to another, commonly called the "monkey mind." Just observing and then coming back to the breath enables the raising of one's consciousness. Vipassana, also known as insight meditation; zazen; and the modern mindfulness meditation all use a form of breath meditation.

LOVING-KINDNESS

One example of incorporating mantra, visualization, and breath is the practice of Metta, or loving-kindness meditation. This supports the meditation practice through many levels of our being. You can do a loving-kindness meditation while either seated or walking. If you choose to add in walking, this then makes for an all-encompassing form of these techniques.

Loving-kindness is defined as unconditional kindness and friendliness. The practice in its simplest form usually entails the sending of loving-kindness and "breaking down of barriers":

- *Toward self*
- *Toward someone close*
- *Toward someone you know*
- *Toward a hostile person*
- *Toward everyone everywhere*

As we mentioned at the beginning of the chapter, we do not present here all of the various styles and techniques. Our hope is that we have shared enough information to interest you (wet your appetite) in starting your investigation into styles and techniques that resonate with your life. They all present opportunities for setting an intent of not only empowering your growth but also supporting others in their quest for a more balanced life. May you find that which brings out your best and enables it in all those you encounter.

Stop
Pause
Think positive
Be an optimist
Today will be a great day

NOURISHING MIND AND BODY

*"You are the only person
who thinks in your mind"*
– Louise Hay

As holistic nutrition professionals, Mira and Kerry both work with a range of clients, helping them create a unique nutritional plan to meet the needs of their bio-individual bodies. We teach them more than how to modify their diet. We address the philosophy of holistic wellness: looking at the whole person and how to support and balance wellness from multiple angles.

Our modern culture tends to encourage a focus on one aspect of wellness at a time, such as food, physical movement, or spiritual wellbeing. Rarely do we incorporate wellness practices that support our emotional side. Almost never do we focus on mind, body, and spirit—the whole, holistic aspect of who we are and what we need to be healthy. We are whole beings who function better when we have balance in all facets of ourselves.

Other important body support practices include restorative sleep, balancing our thoughts and our emotions, and finding time to develop mindfulness and clarity. If we think of them at all, these things tend to be last among our priorities. Sadly, we abandon many of these critical self-care habits when we are under stress, just when we need them most.

While we cannot eliminate the stressors in our lives, we can be mindful of the root causes and form a deeper awareness of our instinctive reactions to it. Without practice, most of us tend to react strongly and negatively to unexpected stressful events.

Once we develop a regular meditation or mindfulness practice, it is possible to learn to balance and temper those reactions and the negative self-talk. If we break down those stressors and take the time for a daily mindfulness practice, we are better able to avoid getting knotted up over the things we cannot change. We are practicing self-care and encouraging the habit of patience along with building a mindfulness routine.

There is a strong mind-body connection. When we focus on one and exclude the other, it can be difficult to achieve all of the changes and goals that we've set for ourselves. Just as we want to nourish the body, to feed it healthy foods, stay well hydrated, and avoid negative ingredients, so, too, we do best when we nourish the mind. Adding in a practice, any practice really, helps create a shift in our mental patterns and allows us to change gears, even if just for a little bit. Taking a break from thinking, from all of the mindless chatter and the overwhelming mental dialog, frees up some mental space and energy. That, in turn, feeds us, perhaps opening up pathways to creative thought or even just calming the body state. When we soothe our thought process, we open ourselves up to more positive thought energy, to letting go of many of the pressures that build up a little at a time without being aware of it.

Often when engaging in some form of meditation, most people find that there is a distinct physical change that goes along with it. Their blood pressure goes down, or their shoulders relax. They can take a deep breath and feel less anxious; they even sleep better. They may find that their stomach doesn't hurt. There's a connection between the body and the brain. Oddly enough, the stomach is sometimes referred to as the "second brain," and high levels of mental or emotional stress can cause stomachaches. There's no medicine for that, but learning to nourish the mind and redirect thinking can calm these gut reactions.

In a way, nourishing the mind by incorporating some form of meditation puts your brain on a mini-cleanse. Most meditation practices are quiet ones. Our modern life is always on, connected, so noisy, out-loud, and overwhelming that we truly need that quiet to settle down and refocus. We crave the ability to have that peacefulness but have gotten so sidetracked by the volume of everyday living that we have forgotten how to reclaim and settle into that silence.

Of course, not all practices are quiet. Some are highly energetic and offer an opportunity to expose your wild side. You can let go and embrace the high-energy output as a form of release. When you do this, you're letting go of the inner critic and embracing a modified state of being that allows for a mental and emotional shift. You're freeing yourself, even if just for just a short period, from the weight of your worries.

Because there is such a deep connection between mind, body, and spirit, it's important to develop a sense of mindfulness. To become aware of the sensations of the breath, the physicality of the body, and observing thoughts in your mind non-judgmentally. To be aware of multiple aspects of who we are and what we need to support the entire bio-individual body. Our four-point practice for whole body wellness is quite simple:

1. *A nourishing diet:* Eat seasonal, organic, unprocessed, local foods as much as your budget and availability will allow. Being sure to incorporate colorful whole foods that are free of chemicals, pesticides, additives, and other unhealthy ingredients. A healthy diet includes more alkaline foods, utilizes all of the tastes (sweet, sour, salty, bitter, pungent, and astringent), and adds in booster foods (seeds, spices, herbs, and nourishing liquids). Please be mindful of and grateful for your food. Digestion starts with the eyes. You nourish the body fully when you take a deep breath, slow down, and focus on the food in front of you. Then you can eat with an appreciation for your food.

2. *Move your body:* Engage in some form of exercise, something that gets you up off the sofa or out of bed and moving. You don't need to run an Ironman race, but you do need to move. Dance by yourself in your living room, take a walk around the block, swim, take an exercise class. Find what works for you and practice it regularly.

3. *Sleep*: We all need more Vitamin Zzzz. Modern society has us convinced that if we can get by with less sleep, we're superheroes. Most of us need far more than we're getting. And modern technology isn't helping. Lights,

computers, smartphones, and televisions are distracting and stimulating. They emit blue light. Short, high-energy wavelength light which is the wrong lightwave for restful, restorative sleep. Fasting from, or avoiding, blue light can support deeper sleep. Start with a thirty-minute blue light fast before bedtime. If needed, increase this to sixty or ninety minutes before bedtime. For some people, it may even be necessary to remove any electrical devices from the bedside near the head.

4. *Get Mindful:* A meditation or mindfulness practice is crucial to good health. It allows you to feel calmer and less stressed, and it supports that mind-body connection. By learning how to engage that aspect of self, you can begin to let go of negative thoughts and emotional patterns. You decrease stress hormones and their impact on the body. You also open yourself to greater possibilities for positive energy and thoughts.

It's important to remember that these changes don't happen overnight. When getting started, it's easy to get off-track or to feel overwhelmed. Just as when you start a new diet, there are habits and thought processes that need to be unlearned. So it is with building and embracing a mindfulness practice. It may start out great, but then you get distracted. Or your tell yourself you're not "doing it right." We're here to tell you there is no right or wrong. If whatever mindfulness practice you're doing feels good and is something you can sustain, then you're doing it right.

This book is about making this process accessible to everyone. It's about encouraging baby steps. Each time you practice meditation, each time you soothe and support that side of your being, you are doing one more thing than you were doing before. You're nourishing that aspect of you. Don't give in to your inner critic. Muscles that haven't been exercised in a while (and that includes mindfulness muscles) may be achy or stiff when you first start out. But the more you practice, the easier it gets.

Strength may not require holding on
It may mean letting go

MOVING THROUGH EXPECTATION

"When I let go of what I am,
I become what I might be"
– Lao Tzu

Consciously or unconsciously, we feed ourselves messages all the time. Many are expectations. Those internalized thoughts, realistic or not, become crystalized and then filter through our daily lives to influence us.

These expectations drive us to seek validation from situations, settings, and others around us. They are the undercurrent of our relentless drive for external approval. And while we may from time to time achieve outside validation, somehow it never feels like enough. It doesn't fill the inside, and so we're left questioning what happened, feeling awkwardly unsettled, and wondering why we don't feel better.

Often we silently set expectations for ourselves. However, much of the time and without meaning to, we assign the origin of our expectations to others in our lives. But because we are the ones who have created them, and because those other people in our lives are not living inside our minds, we frequently wind up creating a rigid, overwhelming process where none need exist. We then follow this train of thoughts and feelings, consciously or unconsciously, in such a manner that it creates stress in our lives.

The incessant chatter and noise of the mind, sadly, is the antithesis of mindfulness. That monkey mind chatter lives in the back of our thought process. A subtle, inaudible rumble runs beneath conscious awareness—non-stop thought that leaves us feeling uncomfortable and unsatisfied. But the rumble isn't real. It is an artificial construct we have created. We made it up!

As we work toward creating a deeper sense of mindfulness in our lives, that noise and the resulting stress can and does subside. This does, however, require work which can be an uncomfortable process. Moving through expectations can be challenging, in part because we need to learn to recognize them for the shadows on the edges of our consciousness that they are. We must sit with the discomfort we often feel when facing our expectations head-on before we can let them go and move forward.

Part of the challenge with expectations is that often we don't verbalize them to those we have assigned them to: a parent, a child, a lover, a boss or co-worker, a neighbor, etc. We hold them silently inside ourselves, believing them to be true. We reinforce them in subtle ways, never realizing how they are obscuring the clarity we need to experience those calmer, more peaceful, more mindful moments we are seeking.

So how do we begin to move through these serenity-crushing expectations?

First, we develop the habit of acceptance, learning to "be with what is." We attempt to simply understand, to clearly see that situations and people may not be what we expect, but they are not necessarily wrong. The more rigidly we hold to a particular expectation, the more challenging it can be to simply let go. When we accept situations and people for what they are, when we recognize that things just are (not right or wrong) and release expectations, we will experience much less frustration. In turn, we create more of that gentle space within us that can generate those moments of mindfulness.

Mindfulness is the willingness to be open, to be aware, to be present. And it's not easy. We get caught up in our demands, our expectations (real or imagined), our singular focus, leaving us with a sense of frustration and disappointment. Rigid thoughts and desires hinder flexibility. How many times in your life have you looked back at a situation that seemed overwhelming, that was fraught with negative emotion and felt so hard, so challenging? And when it was over, you realized the outcome was exactly the right thing, especially if it was one you had not anticipated, How much easier would that transition have been if it had been approached mindfully, with acceptance and flexibility? How difficult did you make things for yourself by holding on to your expectations?

Of course, it's difficult not to have expectations, even the ones that are frustrating and that induce panic. They're subtle. They infiltrate our thinking and color our emotions without our awareness. And if we do recognize them? If we do try to let go of them? It can be its own sort of panic. We're so used to swimming in a sea of expectation that letting go and moving through the expectation feels almost naked and very uncomfortable.

There's a beautiful lyric from the Leonard Cohen song Anthem that we believe illustrates the benefit of letting go of expectations:

> *"Forget your perfect offering*
> *There is a crack in everything*
> *That's how the light gets in."*

Those hairline spaces where we nervously learn to let go and move through, those are the cracks. The growing sense of mindfulness and calmness? That's the light. By incorporating small, regular practices of mindfulness and meditation, we let in the light by creating more cracks.

Lest you think that Mira and Kerry live perfectly serene, untangled, uncomplicated lives, be assured that's not the case. While finding time, space, and creating habits to aim for that, we both recognize that sometimes messy things in life are just that: messy. We both recognize that life is a journey; that building a meditation practice and letting more mindfulness into our lives creates space and clarity. But make no mistake, it is an on-going process. We try to exercise our mental and emotional muscles on a regular and consistent basis. Getting to a more mindful life and finding a meditation practice that works is a process and one that we both work on every day.

The Discover Meditation chapter describes ways that you can add one or more types of meditation to your life. The Workbook section has exercises and prompts you can use. Additionally, many friends and colleagues have shared practices that work for them. Meditation is not a one-size-fits-all kind of thing; some practices may work for you others may not.

Experiment and experience until you find a practice that is comfortable, where your light shines through. Please be kind to yourself. As human beings, we are perfectly imperfect. We find balance through experiential learning. Unless we've been through the trials and tribulations, we cannot fathom or even appreciate the success of releasing tensions and expectations. We may not recognize what it feels like to put down the burden of expectation until we've been weighed down by it. In letting go and moving through expectations, there is no right or wrong way to build your mindfulness practice, because this sort of thing is highly individual. It needs to work for you, your brain, your emotions, your state of being. Remember to let go and move through. It's not about perfection; it's about progress.

Start where you are. Breathe deep. Let go.

*A single kind word or action
can change someone's entire day*

KERRY'S MEDITATION

"Mindfulness is a pause
It's the space between reaction and response
That's where choice lives"

For me, the word "meditation" used to conjure up a mental image of a cross-legged person sitting still in a quiet, serene, peaceful place. While this is the method of choice for many who meditate, I've learned there are many modalities of meditation from which to choose and practice.

I've been on a meditation journey since my early 30s, and I can honestly characterize myself as not that mental image – at least not all the time! My meditation practice came to me slowly over the years via my physical practice of yoga, which at its essence readies the body for meditation. I've had the great joy and honor of studying with some amazing teachers and have been exposed to many modalities of meditation from mantra to mindfulness to sensory and others. The form that resonates with my body, mind, and spirit is experiencing my life as a meditation. This means being mindful in the moment and experiencing all that moment has to offer. The practice of mindfulness meditation resonates with me, because my life philosophy is: "What goes in shows up.™" Everything we see, smell, taste, hear, touch, think, and believe can have a profound effect on the mind, body, and spirit. This belief is at the foundation of the work I do every day in my wellness practice. I'll share a couple of personal examples with you.

Each day my meditation practice takes a different form, depending on what is needed of me at the time and to what experience I'm responding. For me, "respond" is the key word. The practice of meditation has provided me the tools and opportunity to live in response to life rather than in reaction to situations.

I want to live from a place of calm rather than a place of stress or life "happening" to me.

I begin each day with a meditation on a thought, intent, and purpose for my day. I then share this with others on my Facebook page. I call it my "practical inspiration" post. I try to share an inspirational or motivational quote along with a question that allows a brief pause to reflect in an otherwise full day. A question I often share is, "How are you cultivating happiness in your life today?" as I sit with this question myself. Here is my humble answer:

Every day, I look forward to being in my day because I know that I'm going to come into contact with amazing people – from individual clients to meeting people in places I frequent, to friends, family, community, and to speaking engagements and classes I get to teach, etc. With each encounter, there is something to learn (thank you!) and share (hopefully! – from the smallest gesture of a smile to a long, in-depth conversation.

I have yet to find the words to adequately express the joyful and inspirational feelings I get in the presence of people sharing their gifts with the world. So I try to remember to say this little prayer every day: "May we all continue to shine brightly for ourselves and each other. May we each remember to give without remembering who gave to us, and may we receive without forgetting from whom we received."

I wrote this to remind me to respond rather than react to my situation and circumstances: "Mindfulness is a pause. It's the space between reaction and response. That's where choice lives."

Another form of meditation I use is one of being mindful of the words I choose to use. I work with people every day leading classes, workshops, speaking engagements, one-on-one consultations, etc. I want to use language that inspires abundance rather than lack. For example, I like to use the word "options" rather than "modifications" when I provide guidance in a movement class. To me, the word "option" gives my students permission to do what's needed for their body that day rather than thinking they have to "modify" because they can't do a particular movement. Also, I do my best not to tell a nutrition client they "can't" have something. Instead, I focus on all the things they can have and let the less-than-beneficial options fall by the wayside on their own. For me, delivery of the message is key.

When I was very young, I began a ritual of a private "letting go" meditation every New Year's Eve day. I choose to let go of or replace a word in my vocabulary that no longer serves my life's purpose, that might hold me back from reaching my highest potential, goals, dreams, hopes, helping others, etc. For example, words I've let go of include: hate, gossip, ignore, weak, ugly, avoid, fail, unworthy, comparison, competition, modification, jealousy, doubt, can't, fear, worry, and should.

The word I let go of last year is "busy." Is my day busy or full? Am I using being busy as an excuse to myself and others, for not doing the important things, the scary things, or the difficult things? I've been asking myself these questions a lot this year. It seems to me that in our high-tech, low-touch culture, we're finding ourselves continually switched on, connected, overbooked, stressed, and trying to keep up with too many tasks and commitments on our plates. Our culture places a great deal of value on being "busy." The busier we are, the more valued and valuable we think we are. But are we?

The word "busy" connotes drudgery; monotony; drained; how fast can I get things done; how much can I pack into a day to feel worthy; and days filled with things I have to do rather than what I want to do. I need a better word to describe my day! I love what I get to do every day, and saying "I'm busy" just doesn't give it justice.

Instead of saying "I'm too busy," I prefer to convey that my day is full. The word "full" sets the tone of feeling satiated; complete; less frantic; less demanding; a rich life; fulfilled; on purpose; looking forward to my day; energy; sharing; showing up in life vibrant and excited!

I love this Zen proverb: "You should sit in meditation for twenty minutes every day – unless you're too busy; then you should sit for an hour." It conveys what meditation is all about. I ask myself, "What do I truly value?" "Am I effective?" "Can I live in the moment?" "Do I set reasonable expectations?" "Am I ready to stop looking at my day as being 'busy' and start enjoying the 'fullness' of my life so I can make space for more of my vibrant energy to shine through?"

This yearly ritual has allowed me to set a tone and to create positive space for new things to enter my life and to create a more grounded energy to move through the world no matter the circumstances that cross my path. That doesn't mean I don't have tough times. It means I now have more energy to help me move through tough times, and I have even more energy to appreciate the good times and to help others.

I consider myself a lifelong student of yoga. It's at the core of everything I do in the world including the gift of cultivating a daily meditation practice. As my practice has deepened over the years, it has helped me tremendously to move from an "external" to an "internal" practice. At the time I began this journey no one could have prepared me for what would happen as a result of my practice. My practice has not only given me a longer, leaner, more flexible body; it has helped me to discover who I am and to reconnect with my spirit through the practice of meditation.

Appreciate each new day,
seek new horizons,
add light to your inner spirit

KERRY'S 'PRACTICAL INSPIRATION' MEDITATION

One form of meditation I use is to begin each day sharing a 'practical inspiration' meditation posting with my readers. I also provide a question that relates to the posting to allow the reader to briefly pause in an otherwise full day and reflect.

Here are two examples of my 'practical inspiration' meditation posts:

My personal daily affirmations…

"Think positive, be an optimist. Say to yourself every morning:
Today is going to be a great day.
I can handle more than I think I can.
Things don't get better by worrying about them.
I can be satisfied if I try to do my best.
There's always something to be happy about.
I'm going to be apart of helping someone be happy today.
Life is awesome; make the most of it."

What is your affirmation for today?

Breathe…

"Practice being in the moment.
Breathe slower, walk slower, talk slower, respond after careful consideration,
ask thoughtful questions, be still and listen. What a privilege it is to be alive,
to breathe, to think, to enjoy, to love.

Take in that moment. That's when you realize what you authentically want
and truly need. It's also what your heart truly doesn't want and what
your soul doesn't need. It's not always about finding yourself, but creating
yourself because you want something different.
Sometimes the change is by choice, and sometimes it's not.
When you try to control everything, you enjoy nothing.
Sometimes you just need to relax, breathe, let go and live in the moment."

How are you taking time to breathe into the moments in your day?

Meditation is simply the
act of being "me-sponsible"
for your own inner peace

MIRA'S MEDITATION

*"If it weren't for my mind,
my meditation would be excellent"*

– Ani Pema Chodron

I'm one of those people who love the traditionally held idea of meditation: quieting the mind, sitting still, and clearing the mindless monkey chatter out of my brain. I truly do like the idea of it. But the practice? Not so much.

Over the years have I tried and failed so many times at stilling my mind. At reaching for that calmness, the nothingness that I was assured would bring bliss once I learned to master it. I tried it on my own with meditation-superior friends telling me all I needed to do was practice. Eventually, I decided I needed a class. I liked the people and the conversation. But once we got to the quiet part I got...well, honestly, bored. And I would sit there pretending, occasionally peeking just a little bit at all those people sitting around me looking like they were in deep meditative thought. All I could think was, "Darn they look so peaceful, I wonder how they do that?" or "How long has it been?" or "Did I remember to shift the laundry from the washing machine to the dryer?" As a last resort, I would mentally build my grocery list and decide that maybe I should stop at the store on the way home. As for the attempt to still my mind? All it brought me was frustration, the conviction that I was hopeless at meditation, and the sneaking suspicion that everyone else was "getting it" except me.

I'm not a particularly quiet person. Fairly energetic, highly communicative, and frequently going in three or more directions at once, I even have several books at a time going on my nightstand. It's no wonder that I was seeking the stillness of a meditative practice. But finding balance through stillness? I just couldn't figure out how to get there, even when I had people to teach me.

Eventually I found other people who were similarly unable to connect and find peacefulness using stillness as a form of meditation. There was a sort of camaraderie and joy in discovering that we all felt the frustrations of not being able to "get it." We were seeking something; we weren't sure what it was, but we knew this wasn't it for us.

Today, people seem to equate meditation with that form of finding perfect stillness. Now and then there's even some news article talking about "the happiest man in the world" (who is a Buddhist monk who meditates a lot – by 2015 Matthieu Ricard had achieved 10,000 hours of meditation). But if that's the standard we're holding ourselves to, I think it may be difficult to realize. Against that measure, the idea of finding a meditation practice becomes frustrating and overwhelming. Eventually, I learned that I didn't need to do that. As much as I love the idea of attaining that quiet stillness, possibly even while sitting in lotus pose, I finally recognized it probably wasn't going to work for me.

I learned that building a rewarding meditation practice is a matter of finding the form of meditation that would work best for me. There are many forms of meditation, and none is "better" or superior to another.

Learning this was very exciting to me and led me to try other types of meditation. You'll read about different forms of meditation and how they are practiced later in this book. But for now just know that, while I haven't tried them all, I've tried a number of them and found one that works well for me now.

Breathing meditation was not too bad. I found myself able sometimes to sit and just focus on my breath. I discovered, however, just as with the stillness meditation, my thought waves started overwhelming my desire just to focus on my breath. The few moments of quiet I achieved were lovely, but thought bubbles rising to the surface overshadowed whatever momentary stillness I achieved.

I've tried journaling as a form of meditation. The idea was very appealing, but the discipline to journal every day eventually proved to be too much. Countless times I would start a new journal, delighting in the beauty of blank pages and with grand ideas of filling them. I tried various types of journaling: free form, gratitude, scripted, story. Usually, one of two things happened. I either ripped out the pages and threw them away (leaving lots of falling apart, tatty-looking journals), or I put the journal away. And then later I would find it and start up again, sometimes with years in between one entry and the next. I really wanted to be able to do this, but over I time came to accept that again, this was not the right form of meditation for me.

Eventually, I found my way to a yoga class. That was a lot of fun. I got to move my body and stretch while listening to peaceful music that enhanced the experience. I loved my yoga teacher and her calming, gentle voice. Best of all was when we got to the end of our practice. We all lay down on our mats, put on our socks, covered ourselves with a blanket, put on an eye pillow, and went into shavasana, the corpse pose. My body felt delightfully floaty and my mind was (finally!) at ease. I enjoyed it so much that I began practicing yoga at home. And while the home sessions weren't quite as peaceful as the sessions at the studio, they were calming. Yoga enabled me to de-stress from my busy, active life. Yoga, I decided, was my meditation practice. And it was a good one.

Then about fifteen years ago, when I was living in Connecticut, I experienced a very difficult health challenge. I had so little physical energy that I had to abandon my yoga practice. The transitions and some of the more vigorous movements left me so fatigued that I could only lie on my mat in child's pose. I could hardly justify paying for a class when I was just going to lie there curled up on that mat (no matter how sweet the music was!). After all, I could do that at home. But I didn't do it at home, and eventually, my yoga practice faded. The mat sat, rolled up, in the corner of the closet to gather dust. With it went the little bits of serenity that I had acquired through learning this practice, just when I needed it most. It didn't seem fair.

When a friend of mine built a brick labyrinth in her backyard, she invited me over to walk it. She built it because walking meditation is her favorite practice, and she absolutely loves walking the pattern. She was very enthusiastic about this form of meditation and assured me that I would love it. So I went over for a cup of tea and a trial walk. It was nice, but it didn't strike me as very calming or meditative. Plus I couldn't see driving all the way to her house every time I wanted to meditate. On to the next thing.

Then I found passage meditation. You memorize a spiritual poem, scripture, or prayer and repeat it over and over in your mind for as long as you want to meditate. I joined a group where we had readings, discussions, and then a thirty-minute meditation. This was a little easier for me because I had something I could focus on. Again, I enjoyed the company of the other people in the group. I even memorized a r-e-a-l-l-y long passage that appealed to me on a lot of different levels. I truly appreciated the quiet moments of the class. Repeating my passage seemed to help me stay more focused and get to that point of clarity. I also practiced at home, even though the energy seems stronger when you meditate with others. My home practice was enjoyable and calming, but somehow I wasn't able to go as deep into that relaxed stillness as when I practiced with the group. Eventually, time constraints required me to leave this group. Once I left, my ability to continue this form of meditation dissipated into nothingness.

Rather than becoming discouraged that I could not seem to continue with a practice, I began looking for a new type of meditation that might work for me. I wasn't giving up on anything; I was just seeking a better fit. I realized that just as there is no one perfect form of meditation, what we need in a meditation practice changes over time. For some people, it may be different from day to day. Others may stick with a single form for decades or their entire lives. The important thing is to recognize what is and isn't working and to be open to change. Seek a new modality that will support your mind-body balance.

Meditation snuck into my life, too, in quotidian moments of simple, repetitive chores. When my children were young, one of my favorite things to do was to hang laundry on our covered, screened-in porch. It was just me and the laundry. I found peace hanging each piece on the line, perhaps bringing another basket or two after I hung the first basket of clothes. I would come back after the clothes dried to take the laundry down, folding each piece as it went into the basket. Of course, I'd hold the sheets and t-shirts up to my face, relishing the lovely, fresh smell of soap and sun. Admittedly, some days the weather wouldn't be pleasant. But, even if the day was hot or chilly, there was still something special about that quiet time, just me and the laundry.

We've since moved to Texas. I've not found the desire to hang laundry here because it's too hot and humid (and the homeowners association frowns on it). But I've created another quotidian moment that lends me a quiet bit of grace. I treasure the lovely early mornings when I can go out on my covered breezeway, still in pajamas, with a cup of tea. I curl up in a chair and look out over the backyard to appreciate the ever-changing scenery of the seasons. It's only ten to fifteen minutes, but when I am able to take that time, it's deeply satisfying and sets the right tone for the day.

We move so quickly that we forget about, ignore, or miss the serene moments sprinkled throughout the day. As we recognize these moments and focus on them, we can build a deeper awareness and appreciation for them and welcome more of those moments into our lives. That mindfulness is in itself a form of meditation. And it's taught me that we don't have to do just one form of meditation.

I recently had the experience of a group meditation that was a very energetic form called Guided Embodiment Meditation. I had never experienced anything like it and found myself blown away. It started with the entire group standing and just swaying, gently and rhythmically, to the soft, guiding voice of the leader and a low undertone of music. Slowly but gradually the leader guided us to more movement and more energetic output. By the end the only way I can describe it was that we were a room of whirling dervishes, and the entire space pulsed with energy. It was exhilarating and freeing. I felt like I was in an altered state.

I confess when we started I felt kind of goofy. I wasn't sure what we were going to do, or if I would like it. Under the skillful guidance of the leader, I found myself diving right in and really getting into it. The beauty of this particular meditation experience was the fact that it was in a large group setting, and a very skilled practitioner led it. At the end of the exercise, I was breathless, buzzing with energy, and I felt great. But this is not the kind of thing that I could see myself doing at home, even with a video to follow.

So what is my favorite form of meditation? I call it "doodle meditation." I doodle in notebooks and journals. In fact, I doodle just about any piece of paper in front of me! I tend to have a couple of regular journals, my favorite places to doodle.

I doodle the most in the one on my nightstand. It's the larger of my two doodle journals, so the pieces that are in it tend to be a little more involved and complex. I love to practice my doodle form of meditation first thing in the morning while I'm drinking a cup of tea. The house is usually quiet and peaceful, and it's a great way to engage my brain and stop me from jumping into full-brain gerbil wheel mode. I also doodle at bedtime; it helps me to calm down at the end of the day and get my brain off that gerbil wheel.

I also carry a small 3" x 5" journal with me in my purse or travel bag so that I have it with me wherever I go. When the mood strikes me, I can pull it out and jot down a quick doodle or add to one that I've started. It's fabulous for those long lines at the Department of Motor Vehicles. I never know what I'm going to doodle. I just pick up a pen and begin. Each page is different from the others; there's no judgment, no specifics, no theme. I give myself no time limit. Sometimes I will doodle pages in series, experimenting with the same shape in different expressions.

Every time I start to doodle, especially in those long-line-waiting-patiently-impatiently situations, it's a great stress reliever. I don't carry around a blood pressure monitor, but since any form of meditation is good for lowering blood pressure, I'm certain doodling is too. I believe that's part of why it's so enjoyable. You can let go of some stress, lower your blood pressure, and mindfully disconnect, all at the same time.

I used to doodle a lot as a child and even into young adulthood. I'm not sure why, but somewhere along the way I stopped. Maybe when I grew up, the demands of adult life made doodling seem, childish. A couple of years ago I rediscovered doodling and began again. The more I doodled the more I realized that it was calming and helped me to stop that monkey-mind chatter. When I'm doodling my mind sort of floats; it's highly meditative and stress-relieving. Putting pen to paper for as many or as few pages as it takes, I just let go and let the doodles flow.

I tend to doodle in black and white. I find that's easiest because all I need is some paper and a pen. Occasionally I will doodle in color, but I really do prefer the black and white version. The best thing about doodle meditation is that there is no right or wrong way to do it.

Coloring books for adults probably have become so popular because they offer a form of doodle meditation. You pick a color, or not, put pen or pencil to paper, and let the creativity flow: calming, centering, focusing on the paper in front of you and your artistic expression. There's also a form of doodling called "zentangles" where you make specific shapes and combine them to make forms and designs. My preference is for free-flowing doodling, but they are all valuable forms of meditation. However you doodle, whether it's free form (you could make your own coloring book pages if you wanted to) or a little more structured, I encourage you to give it a try.

Meditation is not meant to be a forced thing. If we're forcing it, then it often becomes a chore. We can practice as much, as often, and with as many different types of meditation as we choose. We simply need to be aware of what we need and how it fits into our lives. Gentle, regular practice eventually becomes sustaining, supportive, and enjoyable. Open yourself up to the possibilities. There are so many different forms of meditation that if one isn't working or isn't comfortable, just try a different one. Until I tried it, I never imagined a "whirling dervish" activity would be a meditation!

Some days we're completely tapped out, and it's difficult to hold that peaceful thought process. Or we're just scrambling to stay on top of everything we think we need to do. If your regular practice of repeating a mantra isn't working because your mind is spinning, try a guided visualization or doodling! If you need help with this, use the worksheets in the Worksheet chapter as a guide to get you started and give you different modalities to play around with.

While the truth is that those are probably the moments when you need to stop, even just for five minutes, and find your "quiet place," most of us often rush right past them. It's never easy. It takes practice. I encourage you to learn to be more mindful, to become aware of those moments when you are feeling over the top and out of control. With practice, you will learn how to shift into a more peaceful place. That then makes it easier to build a regular, daily (eventually) practice.

In the simple conscious moment of a breath,
it is possible to set aside self doubt

Find balance
Don't let the judgment of others
stop you from being who you are

FRIENDS AND COLLEAGUES MEDITATIONS

Have you tried to meditate but quit because you "didn't know how" or thought you "were doing it wrong?" Maybe you thought you couldn't do it, and so you just gave up and said, "I tried to meditate, but it's not for me." You're not alone. We wrote this book to show you that meditation is accessible to EVERYONE!

We share our own personal meditation journeys and experiences with you – because if we can do it, you can, too. We also invited some of our friends and colleagues to share their experiences with you. Their stories will show that there are many types of meditation and that such diversity brings accessibility, openness, and strength to a mindfulness practice.

We hope these meditation stories and experiences inspire you to discover, nurture, and share your unique meditation experience.

To experience peace does not imply
that life is always blissful or perfect
It allows you to tap into a calm
state of being in the midst of chaos

AJAYAN BORYS

My interest in meditation began in the spring of 1970, my last year in high school. At that time, I was experimenting with psychoactive drugs, which led to an experience that would change the course of my life. In a word, I dissolved into God.

I can best convey what I experienced that evening by a metaphor: Imagine you are the sun, a vast mass of light and energy a million times the size of the earth. Only instead of light and energy, imagine you were clear light, pure intelligence, pure love, pure bliss. Still, there would be an edge, an end of your being, where you ended, and space began. So imagine you were a trillion suns of pure intelligence, love, and bliss. Even then, there would be an edge, an end to yourself. This state I "experienced" (there was no I, no experiencer, no object of experience) was without end. Infinite pure intelligence, love, bliss, light. And in that infinite expanse, not the slightest stir. Absolute perfect peace.

I emerged from that state imprinted with the following self-evident truths:

1. *What I'd experienced was real. No drug could manufacture Infinity.*
2. *That inexpressible state can be realized and lived, and indeed to do so was the very goal of all existence.*
3. *In order to live that state of Godhead, I would have to purify and change my life. I would have to eliminate all distortions in my being.*

I did change my life. I stopped taking drugs, stopped drinking and smoking, and I left my group of intimate friends who did not see the sense in making such changes. Soon after this, I happened upon a copy of the Bhagavad-Gita. As I read this sacred text of India, I found it so intimately familiar it seemed I had written it. This was more vivid to me than how I feel now when I pick up a book I have written. The Bhagavad-Gita expressed the very essence of my Being. Later I had a similar experience in reading a Tibetan Buddhist manuscript on The Great Liberation through Knowing One's Mind.

I tried to meditate and failed miserably. I needed guidance. My first quarter in college I learned Transcendental Meditation®, and that was the beginning of my meditation career. Since then I've studied and taught various meditation techniques around the world. I've combined the best of what I've learned over the past 46 years in a practice I call Effortless Mind® meditation, a system that efficiently allows anyone to enjoy all the benefits of meditation and even allows those with the necessary dedication to directly experience their innermost, infinite divine Self.

ANIK AND DANIELA BOSE

Our meditation practice was inspired by an intensive two-week "inner-work" retreat ten years ago. Morning and evening guided meditation was an integral part of the curriculum to help individuals become aware and break the conditioned patterns of their egoic behaviors. After the retreat, we maintained our practice of meditating for fifteen minutes at the end of the day. We have created a sacred space in our home for our meditation practice. Our practice consists primarily of silent meditation with a focus on the breath. Meditation calms our minds and allows us to get out of our heads and into our hearts. This makes it easier for us to practice unconditional acceptance in our day-to-day lives and to recognize when we fall off the wagon. It is the simplest tool we know of to strengthen our inner witness, live in the present moment, and avoid the pendulum swing that is the hallmark of today's 24/7 thinking-led lifestyle.

ARLAND HILL

In my years of interaction with patients and discussing ways of relieving stress through meditation, I have come to appreciate the individual nature of this process. What works for one person may only amplify stress for another. Each individual must personally explore the triggers that will assist in centering their mind back to a state of balance. This has been true in my personal journey. I often hear others make mention of enjoying the relaxation of a massage or similar activities, saying how this allows them to disconnect. Such activities don't resonate with me. I have taken a different approach that has enabled me to routinely re-focus my ambitions and align my activities with what is most important in my life.

For me, meditation can be summarized by a single word: "reconnect." When I reconnect with nature, I am at my strongest, spiritually, mentally, and physically. Growing up, I had the good fortune of living in the country. The sounds of nature, the peace of walking through the forest, and listening to only the chirping of birds and the rustling of squirrels were commonplace. Being raised a Christian, I came to appreciate the multiple aspects of this creation and the inherent intelligence that it held, but equally the ways in which the rhythms of nature meshed with me. Reconnecting with nature allows me to tune out the rest of the world. It gives me the down time that I need to focus on those elements that we as humans strive for: humility, compassion, productivity, and connectedness, just to name a few.

One of my most treasured times is running my dogs. All of the beauty of nature and the enthusiasm of such a loyal animal bring everything into focus for me. I see my dogs in their element, enjoying the freedom and liberty to run and chase at will. Just viewing this freedom and reflecting on my personal efforts for it provides liberation that guides decision-making. The sounds of nature embodying the landscape, while producing sounds, quiets outside input. It is this reduction in outside volume that allows the mind to zero in on what is most meaningful. Not only is this critical for the mind and spirit, but it is an essential element of physical growth and regeneration. In recognizing the importance of this need, I even make attempts to artificially create it when possible with recorded nature sounds and being in the proximity of my beloved dogs. With each passing day, my desire for this time with "man's best friend" in the outdoors becomes more cherished and therapeutic.

*In the face of adverse conditions
if you can be with what is
you can survive and grow*

BEDROS KEUILIAN

I tried meditating before; meditating was just not my thing. My ritual involves surfing in the mornings as often as I can. And if I'm not able to get in the water and surf that day, then I take ten, fifteen, or twenty minutes to go over the things I'm grateful for. For me, it comes down to three little things. First, I think of three people whom I'm thankful for that day. Then I come up with three people I want to help that day—maybe it's to make an introduction or a connection for them. And then I think of three people I'm going to text and just puff them up because there's not enough of that going around. Everyone is always cutting other people down, and I believe the best thing we can do as humans is to help each other out. Send them a positive, enthusiastic message. Your morning sets the tone for the rest of the day. Your day sets the tone for the rest of the week. It's as simple as that.

I have found something that works for me. I have now included that as my form of meditation in my daily life practice for decades now. It has brought me overall peace, heightened intuition and connection with my higher self, better health and decreased stress. I've experienced stabilized blood pressure to the point that I no longer need blood pressure medication. When going through difficult times, meditation helps me stay positive and focus on the right things.

CORY ROSS

The year 1999 was a very hard year for me. My marriage was at a low point; I had a bike accident; my mother died; a young girl's car crashed into mine—she died, and I was severely injured. I was undone: how could this happen to her? To me? I lived a clean and wholesome, kind, and generous life. If I couldn't protect her or myself, how could I protect my children? Life was too random, I railed and cried. A friend, a yoga teacher, and a therapist each independently suggested, "You might try meditation."

Although softened by two lovely daughters, I was a million-mile-an-hour, get-it-done type, but I knew it wasn't working this time. So I joined a Vipassana group. As I squirmed through sessions and listened to talks, I began to quiet the screaming voices in my head, getting to know myself, and slowly I healed my body and mind, emotion and spirit.

This was the first venture that I did not research in advance; I just showed up and soaked it in, comfortably sometimes, sometimes not! I spent fifteen years faithfully with a Vipassana sangha, gradually adjusting to silence and retreats, sometimes other traditions: Zen, Tibetan, whatever was available wherever I was, and making my practice my own. I have a personal Vipassana-style practice that I can invoke with a few breaths, bringing me into the moment. I get a lot from shared meditation and sacred environment of some of the local groups in my new town, but I haven't become part of any one group yet.

The benefits of meditation have been many, large, and wonderful: greater peace of mind; enhanced ability to let go of events, troubling and pleasurable; deeper acceptance of what is and being with it; expanded balance of being with doing, and greater empathy with others. I feel more fulfilled in relationships and clearer about what is mine to work with, and what is not!

DON MCCLURE

I started meditation in the 70s when I was participating in a consciousness-raising course. It stuck, and I have been through many meditation styles. I am now comfortable with the Chakra meditation as taught in Ajayan Borys's book Effortless Mind.

I like to tell young people that they can change their lives with just five minutes a day of meditation. The daily benefits of less stress and in general "feeling better" provide a more relaxed way of living. It takes more to push my buttons on days that I meditate.

ERIN KNIGHT

My favorite way to get out of my head and be present is salsa dancing. To follow someone's lead requires my absolute attention and that I shut my thinking brain off entirely. It's isn't what most people would call meditation, but after three hours I feel renewed and like my brain has just gotten back from Hawaii.

HALLIE MOORE

I have used Passage Meditation, developed and taught by Eknath Easwaran (Easwaran.org) for nearly thirty years to anchor my day and my life. In this practice, one memorizes a passage from a sacred scripture and repeats it silently during the period of meditation. Not only does this focus the mind, much like other practices use the breath, but it also drives deep into consciousness the enriching meaning of the passage. My favorite passage to memorize first is "The Prayer of Saint Francis." You probably already know it!

Lord, make me an instrument of thy peace.
Where there is hatred, let me sow love;
Where there is injury, pardon;
Where there is doubt, faith;
Where there is despair, hope;
Where there is darkness, light;
Where there is sadness, joy.
O divine Master, grant that I may not so much seek
To be consoled as to console,
To be understood as to understand,
To be loved as to love;
For it is in giving that we receive;
It is in pardoning that we are pardoned;
It is in dying to self that we are born to eternal life.

Besides the silent repetition of a memorized passage, this spiritual practice includes vital life choices, known as the Eight Points. In addition to silent meditation, these points include repetition of a mantram, slowing down, one-pointed attention, training the senses, putting others first, interacting with a spiritual community, and reading the mystics.

Passage meditation has introduced me to the wealth of the wisdom traditions: I have memorized passages from Taoism, Buddhism, Christianity, Judaism, Humanism, and the Hindu tradition. These passages are positive and inspiring, and they encourage me to incorporate their ideals into my life.

Meditation allows you to step into your life

HELAYNE WALDMAN

When I need to get quiet, I visit my tree.
My tree is openhearted, loving, and supportive.
It holds me close and whispers its secrets to me.
I, in turn, share my secrets with it.
It is a giving tree.
It gives me access to the universal, to spirit, to breath.
I am in awe of its stateliness, forgiveness, and patience.
It embraces me in safety.
It is the perfect spot to meditate.

JONAH DAS

I started meditating long before I knew I was meditating. As a boy, I grew up in the country in a volatile and violent house —but a house surrounded by big, beautiful, and seemingly endless woods. No matter how terrifying things would get at home, the woods were always there, as if they were patiently waiting for me—peaceful, changing, alive. And no matter the season or weather, I would head off into those woods alone, to special places I'd found: a clearing in a windy cluster of tall pines, the moss-lined hollow of an old tree, a large flat boulder beneath a small waterfall. I would just sit and breathe and listen—to the birds, the burble of the creek, the sound of leaves dropping through the canopy, or pine needles falling onto the snow. I was far away from everything scary and painful, where no one knew I was, where I was safe, where I could just be for a while. I would sit there for as long as it took to get quiet, then close my eyes and imagine the woods imagining me—a place I'd always been and to which I could always return. And as my breath would slow and whatever awful thing that had driven me into the woods would lose its bite, I could see the madness and confusion of the way I was growing up for exactly what it was: just the way I was growing up. Not my fault, not my choice, not my destiny.

After several years of what I now know to call a "practice," I came to recognize a presence in the woods that wasn't in the woods as much as it was deep within me—that the sanctuary I found out in nature was really a sanctuary within, and I could access it anytime I wanted. This discovery was formalized when I was fourteen years old—when my eighth-grade science teacher introduced me and a few other students to Transcendental Meditation® (which was extremely popular at the time) —but mostly, I think, as a way to calm us teenage boys down in class! A few minutes into our very first "sit," I recognized the terrain instantly: it was the same journey—from outer sanctum to inner calm—that I'd discovered alone in those woods a few years earlier as a scared little boy. Over the four decades since, I have engaged in many types of formal meditation practices, in classes, yoga studios, retreats centers, churches, and synagogues around the world. But I still find the easiest and surest access to those same sensations where I first found them: out walking, alone but not alone at all, in the woods.

KASONDRA JANSSON

Each time we sit in meditation, we weave another thread to our source. Over time, these threads begin to form a bridge. It becomes easier to drop in and let go of our drama. I believe any one-pointed focus can be a meditation. For me it is yoga. Art, sports, keeping attention on breath throughout the day, any concentrated effort is beneficial. When the going gets tough, meditation creates a refuge, a place within and under the ever-changing appearances of life. The more we nurture and feed and place our attention on this retreat within, the easier it is to access it. It holds us like a mother who can never die. It is the only permanence in an impermanent world, the only lasting security. We spend more time thinking about our lives than living them. Don't miss it. When my best friend was dying, the only regret she voiced to me was that she wished she had meditated more. Meditation is our companion at death.

KEESHA EWERS

When I was diagnosed with rheumatoid arthritis (RA) in the 1990s, I was confronted with what conventional medicine called an "incurable" chronic disease. Because my grandfather had RA, my doctor told me this was a genetic issue and handed me a prescription for a cancer-fighting drug called Methotrexate. When I looked up the side effects, I knew this was not my path. Instead, I did my research. I found that there were several studies with evidence that meditation and yoga were efficacious for calming autoimmune disease. So I started studying both.

Once I started meditating, my mental reactivity calmed, which led to a calming of my immune reactivity. One day in meditation, a man appeared to me. He showed me a mountain. Later, I found the man and the mountain in a book I was given. His name was Ramana Maharshi, and the mountain is called Arunachala, in southern India. I traveled to India and hiked Arunachala, eventually winding up in the cave Ramana Maharshi meditated and lived in for many years. I sat down in the cave and felt my body evaporate into what felt like flames. Wisdom that was beyond my experiences downloaded into me, and this is much of what I write about and teach today. The path of meditation not only healed my autoimmunity but placed me in the flow of my life's purpose.

KIRSTIN NUSSGRUBER

I fell into the common category of always wanting to meditate, even investing in books and online courses, but never committing to an intentional and consistent practice. Time and a million other things always seemed to get in the way. And then I was diagnosed with breast cancer, and everything changed. It was my wake-up call to show up for myself intentionally, regardless of my schedule. I intuitively knew that this was the missing link to get in touch with myself and honor my health.

During my active cancer treatments, my head was spinning or foggy, or I felt completely overwhelmed, so I relied on guided meditation to calm me down. Without a guide, I was unable to calm my thoughts to the point of receiving any benefit from my practice. I always felt inadequate and like a failure. Listening to guided words got me through this period with a sense of accomplishment. In that space, I felt utterly at peace with what was going on, knowing it is just something I needed to go through on my path.

Moving beyond cancer, when the pace of life and all its challenges washed over me again, I fumbled for a bit but realized that meditation does not mean me having to sit quietly and try and let those relentless thoughts pass through. For me, it still means allowing myself to be totally immersed in the moment, focusing on one activity and being fully present for that. Sometimes we have to be flexible and adapt to our changing circumstances.

When I walk our new puppy these mornings, I am focused on him. We are constantly in training and it demands my full attention. No other thoughts stand a chance to enter my head! That is a form of meditation. Although it may appear exhausting, by the time we get home, I do feel mentally refreshed and able to tackle the day much in the same way as I did when my older dog allowed me to sit quietly in the early morning on the couch and meditate in the more traditional way. It will be some time before our pup allows me to do that again, and getting up earlier is not an option for me either as I need my sleep. But by being flexible, and realizing meditation takes on different forms, I feel I am accomplishing it regardless of my circumstances.

Meditation grounds me. If I do not meditate, I feel like an uprooted plant swaying in the wind. I can check in with myself and zone in on what requires my loving attention from within, not steered from my head. I connect with Source at times; it feels like I am showered in a warm and comforting glow. Sometimes my body vibrates and gently moves with the force of a Universal energy that just passes through me, letting me know I am but a part of the Whole, like all of us. I simply know I am taken care of, regardless what may happen to me in this lifetime.

KYRIN DUNSTON

My mother had my sister and me trained in Transcendental Meditation® (TM) when we were in high school. She was a diligent meditator and thought meditation would help us be better students. The introduction to TM involved an interesting and precious ceremony that I will never forget. I loved the idea of receiving a mantra that was uniquely mine; that no one else knew. As the one thing I have never told anyone, it remains the most private part of me.

That was almost four decades ago. Over the years I have meditated with varying regularity, mostly off. Whenever I would go through a tough time, my mother would always ask me, " Are you meditating?" After my spiritual awakening in 2004, meditation became a key component of my health regimen, and I always feel better having meditated in the morning. I am more energetic and more centered, and wonderful ideas come to me spontaneously. I am more hopeful and alive. I am more present to myself, my life, and the people in it.

It used to be that meditation was something that I had to do, like working out. Now it is something that I get to do and look forward to doing. Because I have realized the benefits of it over time, I prescribe it for all of my patients and find that the ones who participate experience the benefits. I find that newbies do best with a guided meditation with soft background music. I use these as well, but I am most comfortable with TM.

Meditation is a refuge I can go to when life gets tough. It is like being at the bottom of the sea during a storm. It is quiet, eternal, effortless, calm, and real. It reminds me of who I am: a spiritual being having a human experience. And what is important is this: It helps render seemingly insurmountable life mountains into manageable molehills.

Speaking of which, I think I need to meditate and right-size some mountains I think I am facing!

We gain wisdom and balance through reflection

MARCIA SIVEK

For years, mindfulness was a word in my everyday vocabulary for clients, friends, and family. Did I use it as a call-to-action for myself? No! Not until this past year when running my own business, having an autoimmune condition, and death in the family took its toll. I had to revisit the word "mindfulness" and decided it was time I practice what I preach.

There are three ways I now incorporate meditation into my life daily. I either sit in a quiet room with no distraction and practice at least twenty minutes of mindfulness meditation – typically a body scan technique used by Jon Kabat-Zinn. This allows me to clear my mind and check in with my mood and body. This meditation is great to relieve me of everyday anxiety surrounding business stress. I have realized since incorporating this practice, I am more mindful of my breathing; if I begin to take too many short breaths, I have learned to slow down and breathe deeper.

A second way I meditate is through art, specifically watercolor painting. I try to paint at least thirty minutes every day. Painting is how I wind down after being on the computer, on the phone, or speaking all day. It calms me. I especially enjoy the water-based media for its simplicity, flow, and layering capabilities. Tapping into my creative side has helped me focus throughout the day. I know if I can reward myself with color and creativity at the end of the day, everything else is worth it. On days I cannot paint, I really miss it and notice I am more unsettled.

Thirdly, I take a quiet walk in nature. I don't listen to the radio or podcasts, only the wind in the leaves and the songs of the birds. When I do this regularly, I sleep better and feel more refreshed in the mornings. This is probably my favorite way to be kind to myself. I try to be out in nature like this every day, even if for just ten minutes!

MARGARET FLOYD

I have always been a very high-stress person—goal oriented and tightly wound. It was affecting my health, manifesting in chronic headaches and interrupted sleep. I got to the point where I could never turn off the monkey mind. I learned of the Morning Pages technique one summer while listening to Julia Cameron. I've always gravitated to writing, and so I tried it.

It works like this: first thing in the morning you sit down and write three journal pages, by hand. There's no particular format; you write whatever needs to come out. Some days it was a grocery list, other days it was recording a profound dream, often it was just babble. This exercise clears out the mental cobwebs and gives the monkeys a harmless place to speak. I couldn't believe how soothing it was to get them out of my head and onto the page. Either they quieted right down, or I was able to have a real conversation with them and come up with compelling solutions for issues that had been bothering me for months, sometimes even years.

Not only did this practice ease the stress in my life, but it was also the precursor to some important ideas for me professionally and was a key part of the process in the inception of my first book, Eat Naked. Instead of waking up feeling anxious, I looked forward to this quiet time of sipping a cup of tea and doing my "Pages." To this day, I think of my Pages as a real entity – often asking them questions and thanking them for the insights that come out of the process. It's a beautifully meditative and productive process. I can't imagine life without them!

MELISSA CRISPELL

Meditation. That was an intimidating concept for me at first. In the beginning, I searched for guidance to learn how to meditate because all of my expert peers were telling me this is what I needed to do to become more grounded and focused. In my search to learn how to meditate, I came up with the same instructions over and over. "How to meditate for beginners: all you need is five or ten minutes a day in a quiet comfortable space, become present, become totally aware of your current surroundings, and focus on your breath."

My brain screamed, "WHAT?! Stop what I'm doing? Stop answering phone calls and emails? Stop working? Focus on my breath – I thought I did that automatically?" I thought this meditation idea was crazy talk for a type-A like me, but I tried, because "it would be good for me." It was a struggle for a quite a while. I even quit and tried again a few weeks later (more than once). My brain wanted to wander to my to-do lists; I felt guilty for taking time away from work; I felt like I was lazy and unproductive, and then it all clicked. By taking time for myself, comfortable in the quiet space I created, focused on my breathing, I was setting myself up for even more productivity. I found that if I focus on deep breathing (yes, there is a proper technique) and visualizing every detail of my happy place (the beach), before I know it my time is up, and I feel refreshed and renewed.

I now do this self-care practice twice daily for ten to fifteen minutes at a time; I've decided that I am well worth thirty minutes each day. My body is appreciative as well. I've noticed improvements in my digestion, my emotional responses, my stress level, and my work productivity. My recommendation for beginners is: don't get bogged down in the details. Take one step at a time and, before you know it, you'll be doing it too!

Take time to rest when you need it
Everything will be there when you are ready

MELISSA HUMPHRIES

Meditation has had a profound effect in my quest for personal wellness. I began practicing guided meditation over twenty years ago. It offered me healing from anxiety and mild depression without harmful prescription medications. Throughout my life, I would step away from my practice due to schedule limitations and the hectic demands of my roles of wife, mom, and entrepreneur. It was only a few years ago that I returned to a regular, committed practice. After studying with Deepak Chopra, who was a vital influence on the health-coaching curriculum at the Institute for Integrative Nutrition, I rediscovered the beauty of meditation.

Meditation brings many cognitive benefits and helps me to focus my thoughts and creativity and to manage my busy life. As an Integrative Health Coach, I work with women who are trying to balance their lives in a holistic mind, body, and soul approach. Meditation is an essential ingredient in my "Recipe for Radiance" program. It acts as a foundational detox of the mind to help bring about clarity, confidence, vibrant health, and stress-free living.

Studies have shown that the physiological changes in the body while meditating offer powerful health-promoting benefits. The power of mindful meditation can reduce anxiety, increase focus, increase creativity, reduce pain, reduce depression, decrease blood pressure, reduce inflammation in the body, boost immunity, lower systemic cortisol levels, improve sleep, and offer more balance to our emotions. I often prescribe my clients to "meditate before you medicate."

If you are new to meditation, I suggest following guided meditations that are available online and on YouTube, or apps that are available for smart phones. Eventually, you will discover you can meditate anywhere and anytime. I find quiet music or being in nature is my cue to begin in gratitude, to release thoughts that are weighing me down, focus on slowing my breathing, and reflecting on specific mindful affirmations.

MICHAEL MASTRO

In 1965, through a brief experimentation with recreational drugs, I realized there was more to the one-dimensional mind. I was looking for a natural alternative and was introduced by a friend to Transcendental Meditation. In TM, I discovered much more than a natural high. It was, to me, a natural and graceful system of effortless meditation as opposed to concentration or contemplation. The repetition of the mantra through meditation allows the conscious mind to settle deeply into itself. The mantra is like a springboard that takes one deeply beyond the mind to the source of creation. When the mind settles down, it lets go of all tension and stress and brings us to the present moment. It is only in the present moment that we find true happiness. I have noticed not only less stress from my consistent use of meditation over the years, but also more creativity, improved relationships, and better health.

PAUL REYNOLDS

I've come to the conclusion (for now at least) that the feeling I subscribe to as meditation is a spontaneous occurrence not arrived at by any particular means or style. If there is a characterization that lets me know I am in that space that I would define as meditative, I suppose it would be a loss of a sense of linear time and a sense of peace and connection to all that is a part of my experience here; an acute awareness/completeness perhaps. Words are inadequate of course.

That feeling is often invited in by something as simple as washing the dishes, taking a swim in the ocean, having a heartfelt conversation with someone. (Each of my interviews is a "form" of meditation, I would say.)

The spiritual teacher Krishnamurti came close to expressing it (I'm paraphrasing here) by saying any attempt to systemize meditation is a complete denial of it – much like trying to define the Dharma.

Simply put – my life is my meditation, an attempt to remember a natural state we all possess. It's like trying to define love, I suppose. There are many outward manifestations, but can one ever pin down what it truly is?

RACHAEL PONTILLO

Meditation isn't something that I was taught as a child on purpose. My cousin Barb taught me to repeat the word "nothing" over and over to myself in my mind with my eyes closed when I had trouble falling asleep. Little did I know then that she had taught me my first mantra. No Sanskrit needed. As a teenager I got another exposure at the end of a karate class when we were taught to sit still, eyes closed, and practice deep breathing to calm our bodies down at the end of class. I remember the very first time I deliberately "meditated." It was in my college dorm room my freshman year when my roommate had friends over, and I'll just say it – they were annoying. They were loud and kept bothering me, so I lay down on my dorm bed and closed my eyes. I began to practice the breathing I was taught in that karate class just a few years prior, and I counted out my breaths. I counted my inhales, my holds, and my exhales. Next thing I knew, everyone had left. I had no idea how long I was "out."

I didn't have a regular meditation practice until I was in my mid-twenties and discovered Reiki. Both of the master teachers I studied with offered amazing meditation prompts that were very accessible. One was a simple "Sat Nam" mantra – over and over again – which of course reminded me of "nothing." Another was a pre-recorded guided visualization that I worked with while taking hot salt baths. Today, I use meditation to clear my mind, help get clarity on thoughts or ideas I'm pondering, and to connect with Spirit. (I've seen Buddha, I've seen Quan Yin, I've seen Ceridwen, I've seen the Goddess version of myself, and many faces of the Divine). Sometimes it's ten minutes, and I use a flame to focus; perhaps it's a full-fledged ritual with incense and sound, other times it's a blissful savasana at the end of yoga class, but still today, "nothing" is my go to for helping me fall asleep when my brain doesn't shut off.

The act of clearing my mind through meditation was life-changing for me. It allows me to instantly gain intuitive guidance and improve my mindset in difficult moments (even if I just breathe deeply and count my breaths for a minute), and it's allowed me to clear the mental, emotional, and spiritual cobwebs to make room for positive new thoughts, experiences, and opportunities. Meditation doesn't have to be fancy or lengthy – I always say it's better to work with the time and tools you have and do less more often than to "save up" for a long, elaborate practice less often.

We are all challenged with
something at some point
along the journey of our lives
Choose resilience

ROBIN MASTRO

I had dabbled in spirituality and healing ever since my teens, doing yoga and studying herbology and alternative health before I was out of high school in the late 60s. I studied several spiritual traditions, including Transcendental Meditation, but found my deepest connection to the Divine Source of All That Is through The Art of Living Foundation, combining the techniques of Sudarshan Kriya and Sahaj Samadhi Meditation.

Through Sudarshan Kriya, I can blast out the negative effects of stress that get stuck in the nervous system and within the mind. Then, when I settle into meditation after Kriya, I find I am so much deeper than when I would just sit for meditation. This is so because with the breathing exercises, the mind becomes relaxed and you are literally in the present moment. Without effort, you are just there… the place where the living of your daily life truly exists. So often we fluctuate between our regret and memories of the past and our anxiety and stress about the future; we don't experience the present moment at all. We just don't live fully moment-to-moment because of this vacillation between the past and the future. The Art of Living courses transformed my life and gave me practical tools to live with less stress and more joy every single moment, every single day.

SARICA CERNOHOUS

My journey with meditation began as a result of recognizing I needed to calm down my busy mind and constantly reading that everyone should meditate.... So it was a mix of personal care with societal peer pressure that got me started!

For many years it came in fits and spurts, these half-hearted attempts at meditation, where I would often walk away feeling frustrated and upset with myself for not "doing it right." Thankfully, I found a practice that worked for me. And of course – as many things do – I found it when I was not expecting it. I had joined some dear friends and colleagues for a small group retreat. The spouse of one of our group members just happened to have written a wonderful book on meditation offering a practice that is easy to follow. It has been nearly a year now that I have been using this meditation practice daily. The ease and joy with which I begin every day is absolutely priceless. Where meditation was once a responsibility I couldn't quite master, it has now become a delectable treat I have to pull myself from every morning. My days of full scheduling feel so much more manageable. I'm sleeping better; I'm handling stressful moments more gracefully, and I have an easier time accessing an inner place of peace when I need to. Pretty awesome!

STACY MCCARTHY

I meditate to come home. I have at many junctures in my life sat with the question "what is / where is home?"

When I had my husband at my side, it was wherever we were. It was a state of being. Together was home. After he had passed away, I felt untethered and all over the place. I realized I was living with a constant, low level of anxiety. What's the next shoe to drop?

So I was introduced (again) to meditation.

I used to think I didn't have time to meditate, that it was a waste of time.

Then I started studying somatics, a way of being. Of embodying life. Of aliveness. And meditation is a key enabling practice.

For me, I prefer a walking meditation but have settled into a sitting practice. On my last birthday, a friend 'gifted me 15 minutes'. He sat with me and upped my meditation length from 10 to 15 minutes. He set a new bar for my daily practice. My timer is now default set to 15 minutes. And I try to get to it each day. I don't always get that much, but it's a goal.

The benefit is that I am not as "taken" by what comes my way. I can be at choice in how I respond.

Before it would be a knee-jerk reaction to appease or disassociate. Now I can observe and choose. I hope it can continue to center me and bring me home to myself, to my self-worth, to my dignity, to my sense of belonging. These are human desires that we all have to some degree: safety, belonging, and dignity. When I sit, I recognize that I have them, that a lot is in how I see the world, how I view the world and through what lens am I seeing. When I see, do I see objectively, or through my sometimes-cloudy glasses? Meditation is like a lens cleaner for me. And it takes me home. Home is with me. I have it in me.

TANDY ELISALA

There are many ways to meditate. I've used the following methods most often:

1. *Walking meditation:* This involves the intentional focus on your environment as you walk. Simply BEing with nature is meditative.
2. *Mantra meditation*: This involves repeating a particular word or sounds to get centered.
3. *Listening meditation:* This involves asking a question you'd like an answer to and simply listening for the guidance you get. It could come in the form of recurring thoughts, a splash of inspiration, or a smell, to name a few.
4. *Guided visualization meditation:* This involves listening to a recording of your voice or someone else's with specific topics you focus on.

Meditating even five minutes a day makes a big difference. I encourage you to find a way to meditate that resonates with you and start small. Remember, the conscious mind (the ego) likes to stay busy. When your mind gets sidetracked with thoughts of your to-do list, simply notice your thoughts and redirect your mind. It takes practice to master meditation. Incorporate a meditation practice in your life and experience inner peace and improved health.

Mindfulness isn't about being perfect;
it's about deepening our connection with ourselves

MEDITATION WORKBOOK

WORKBOOK INDEX

Mindfulness Exercises
Pause Meditation
The Power of Five
Raisin Meditation
Quotidian Meditations

Writing Exercises
Gratitude
Highs and Lows
Ten Words
Doodling
Journaling

Breathing Exercises
Alternate Nostril Breathing
Equal Breathing
Progressive Relaxation

Physical Exercises
Walking Meditation
Metta or Loving Kindness
Meditation

For additional copies of the workbook pages found in this book, please visit www.VersadiaPress.com.

You've learned a lot: what meditation is, different forms of meditation, and why incorporating meditative practices into your daily routine is beneficial. Meditation can help you become more mindful and more focused as you move through your day. It can be overwhelming and exhausting to carry the endless chatter of errands, laundry list, what's for dinner, family schedule, etc., just below conscious awareness.

In this workbook, we will talk about how to move through your experience as you build your practice. This is a conscious choice of words as opposed to the more familiar concept of letting go. "Letting go" is something we believe we never fully do. This is because situations that we have moved through are not ones that we ever fully manage to let go of. They become a part of us, an accumulation of our life experience. With time and wisdom, we move through and learn to embrace rather than resist our experiences. But then something happens, perhaps ten years later, and it triggers a return of feeling, emotion, or even physical response. We haven't completely let go. We have, however, learned how to be with a situation so that we have tools that we can use when we encounter it again. We learn to move through and move forward. That's what meditation, or mindfulness, helps us to do.

However moving through a situation can present a challenge unless we take a break or incorporate some form of practice. By adding awareness and focus, it helps us to more fully develop a sense of gratitude, to set our intentions for how we interact with the world around us, and to center ourselves.

Just as we've talked about what meditation is, we need to pause for a moment and talk about developing this sense of mindfulness. Although it can be relaxing for many, mindfulness is not meant to be pure relaxation. Instead, it is a means of focusing on a practice that can help us to let go for just a short time of the crush and chaos that everyday life can sometimes bring. In that letting go for a moment, we are not meant to avoid. Issues that bother us may not impact us the same way, but they are still there. Challenges and problems in our personal lives, at work, or in other areas will still be present. We cannot run away from them simply because we take a few moments to journal, or breathe, or do any other mindfulness practice.

What we learn is to be aware of our discomfort. We discover how to be present and to compassionately evaluate ourselves, the situation or event, and anyone else involved and then to clearly make decisions that are in our best interest. Rather than getting wrapped up our reactions, we open our hearts to embrace the possibilities and respond.

MINDFULNESS EXERCISES

As we've mentioned before, mastery of mindfulness doesn't happen overnight. And it certainly doesn't spring full-blown to the front of your cerebral cortex every time there's something that demands your attention. It takes time and effort. Perhaps you develop a breathing meditation practice that supports you when you are under stress. Or you start your day with doodling to free up your mind, clear the cobwebs of sleep, and flex your intellect and creative spirit for the day ahead. Whatever and however you start and grow with your meditative practice, remember that it's about finding what works and is sustainable for you.

Pause Meditation

This is the practice of stopping whatever you are doing to take a pause and focus on something in your surroundings. (Obviously, we do not recommend this when doing something that requires your full attention like operating machinery, driving, skiing, or hang gliding, etc.) By taking a pause to focus on something (see the examples below), you create a little break for yourself. Shifting for just a moment can help you let go and then come back to whatever you were doing with greater awareness.

The Power of Five

- **Five Breaths**

  Stop what you are doing, relax your jaw, drop your shoulders, roll your head to the left and then to the right. Slowly breathing through the nose, take in a deep breath, filling the belly. Then, breathing through the nose, release this breath. Notice the feeling as your breath comes in, fills your belly, goes out, and empties your lungs. Repeat four more times.

- **Five Sounds**

  Stop what you are doing, close your eyes, relax your jaw, drop your shoulders, roll your head to the left and then to the right. Now sit quietly and note five sounds that you can hear.

- **Five Sights**

  Stop what you are doing and close your eyes for a moment. While they're closed, recognize any light that seeps through your eyelids. Then open your eyes and pick the first five things that catch your attention. Observe them and note details about them that you might have glossed over before you chose to focus on them.

- **Five Sensations**

  Stop what you are doing, Close your eyes, relax your jaw, drop your shoulders, roll your head to the left and then to the right. With your eyes closed, note five physical sensations and connect with your body through these sensations. It could be your feet firmly planted on the floor, the feel of your clothes as they crease around your knees, or the tightness of your jaw. Note what you feel, adjust it if you like, and then continue to the next sensation.

RAISIN MEDITATION

Most of us eat raisins by the handful, scattered over cereal, mixed into trail mix, or from a box as a snack. When you use a single raisin as a tool for focus and mindfulness, you'll be surprised at the array of sensations and interactions you can generate.

Hold the raisin between your index finger and your thumb.
Feel the texture, shape, and squishiness of the raisin.
Then look at it carefully.
Note the color, the wrinkles, and the shape.
Rolling it back and forth, note how that feels and how it changes what you see when you look at the raisin.
Then hold the raisin beneath your nose and smell it.

Is there an aroma that starts to speak to your brain, a smell that is uniquely that of a raisin?

As you smell the raisin, do you experience any other physical symptoms?

Does your mouth water?

Is your stomach reacting?

Now put the raisin in your mouth.

Hold it there, not chewing, but just settling it onto your tongue.

If you'd like, close your eyes to more fully experience how it feels to have the raisin on your tongue.

Is there an increase in saliva?

Is the shape and size of the raisin changing?

Slowly roll the raisin around your mouth, noting the texture as it moves.

Slowly position the raisin so that you can bite it and take one bite.

Holding your teeth closed over the raisin, note how your mouth and body feel.

Take another bite and being to notice the taste of the raisin as the flavor spreads across your tongue.

Very slowly continue to chew until the raisin has become pulpy and soft.

Just before you swallow, focus on the muscles and physical movements involved in swallowing.

See if you can feel the raisin moving down your esophagus and into your stomach.

Now bring your awareness back to your mouth.

Do you still taste the raisin?

Note your feelings and sensations as they relate to the raisin.

QUOTIDIAN MEDITATION

Pick a task or chore. Commit to doing it mindfully. As an example, if you're doing dishes, instead of keeping lots of mindless chatter going while you are loading or unloading the dishwasher, or washing, drying, and putting away the dishes, focus on what you are doing. Notice the temperature of the water, the feel of the dishes. At what point does the dishtowel get soggy? How does the texture of the toweling change the more you use it for the dishes? Notice the space by the side of the sink where you may be stacking dishes. How does it look; how does the light hit that space? What is the temperature of the water? Of the air? Of your skin? Can you feel yourself firmly in the space where you are standing? What sounds accompany your task?

WRITING PROMPTS

Gratitude

Gratitude can be a form of meditation. By focusing on those things we are grateful for, we change our way of thinking. Too often most of us find ourselves thinking more about those things that have influenced us negatively in some way. In doing this, we lose sight of all of the wonderful things that happen as well. By taking just a few moments each day to consciously focus on the positive; to remember and write down something we are grateful for, we teach ourselves to notice more of those moments. Consider keeping a gratitude journal or use the gratitude journal page outlined in the book. Each day, carve out a few minutes, maybe at the end of the day, to jot down a few things you are grateful for that day.

GRATITUDE WORKSHEET

Date: *Gratitudes:*

Date: *Gratitudes:*

Date: *Gratitudes:*

Date: *Gratitudes:*

Date: *Gratitudes:*

Date: *Gratitudes:*

Date: *Gratitudes:*

WRITING PROMPTS

Highs and Lows

This is a modified form of the gratitude exercise. It allows us to acknowledge something that may have happened that was a low for us during the day. However, it also balances itself by also prompting us to think about something that was a win or a high during the day. When we learn to be more mindful of everything that is happening around us, we see that there is balance. Rather than allowing one single moment or event to color our day negatively, we see that our day, our life, is a spectrum. How we experience it and acknowledge it is entirely within our grasp.

HIGHS AND LOWS WORKSHEET

Date: *Highs/Lows:*

Date: *Highs/Lows:*

Date: *Highs/Lows:*

Date: *Highs/Lows:*

Date: *Highs/Lows:*

Date: *Highs/Lows:*

Date: *Highs/Lows:*

WRITING PROMPTS

Ten Words

Ten Words is a writing meditation that encourages free-flowing thought process. Rather than writing a specific thing such as a gratitude or a high and a low, it simply encourages mindfulness for the recollection of your day. There are two ways to utilize this practice. One is to write ten words that describe how you are feeling or how your day was. Write any ten words that come to mind and are meaningful for you. You can also write ten words that express your focus or hopes for the day. The beautiful thing about this exercise is that it doesn't take a long time to accomplish, and it does encourage mindfulness.

TEN WORDS WORKSHEET

Date:

Date:

Date:

Date:

Date:

Date:

Date:

DOODLE PAGE PROMPTS

Doodling is a delightful way to practice mindfulness. Just put pen, pencil, marker, crayon, or what every implement you like to paper to get something, anything down on the page. It's not necessary to complete an image; you don't even need to set a timer (unless you want to).

Sometimes it can be difficult to get started. Staring at that blank page can be intimidating. If that's the case for you, then pick one of these prompts and use it as a starting point. The more you doodle and the more you let your creativity shine, the easier it gets.

- *Circles*
- *Squares*
- *Your name*
- *Flowers*
- *Feathers*
- *Rainbows*
- *A favorite quote*
- *Butterfly*
- *Stars*
- *Triangles*
- *Light*
- *Dark*
- *Mountains*
- *Beach*
- *Meadow*
- *Dreams*
- *Music*
- *Spirals*
- *A letter*

DOODLE PROMPTS WORKSHEET

Date:

Prompt / inspiration:

JOURNAL PROMPT PAGE

You can journal on the next page, or you can write in a notebook or journal each day. Choose the method that works for you: free flowing, timed, or following prompts. Write the same prompt, a different prompt, or make up one of your own. It's simply a matter of choosing what works for you.

There is no right or wrong. You're simply looking to kick start the meditative process of free thought and expressing it through writing. There are several different ways to journal.

Set a timer and write whatever comes to mind for a specific amount of time Write for a specific number of pages, allowing unedited thoughts onto the page Writing an affirmation over and over can be helpful for some people. Here are a few suggestions:

- *I am worthy of being loved.*
- *I embrace myself fully and completely for who I am.*
- *My thoughts and my talents are valuable.*
- *I am beautiful, confident, and worthy of respect.*
- *My body is healthy, my mind is strong, my spirit is calm.*
- *I forgive those who have hurt me and detach with compassion.*
- *I am open to creativity and positive energy as it flows through me.*
- *I choose happiness.*
- *I am courageous and stand strong in the river of my life.*
- *I am ready to leave behind old, negative thoughts and habit to embrace the positive future ahead of me.*
- *I embrace energy and joy.*
- *I am enough just as I am.*

Some people prefer to journal using a prompt to help them get started. Here are a few examples:

- *Today I …*
- *I am grateful for …*
- *I am proud of myself …*
- *A challenge I have overcome is …*
- *Happy thoughts …*
- *Concerns I have …*
- *My favorite …*
- *On my bucket list …*
- *I dream …*
- *Yesterday …*
- *Tomorrow …*
- *I will never forget*
- *30 things …*
- *What I've learned …*
    - *May all beings be at ease…*
    - *I have the strength to…*
    - *My hopes are…*

What we learn is to be aware of our discomfort. We discover how to be present and to compassionately evaluate ourselves, the situation or event, and anyone else involved and then to clearly make decisions that are in our best interest. Rather than getting wrapped up our reactions, we open our hearts to embrace the possibilities and respond.

JOURNAL PROMPT PAGE

Date: *Prompt / inspiration:*

BREATHING MEDITATIONS

Alternate nostril breathing I

This meditation is supportive for the adrenal glands and can help to lower cortisol and blood pressure. It helps to settle the mind, body, and emotions. It helps to balance the right and left sides of the brain, creating whole-brain functioning.

1. *Use your thumb and index fingers to alternately open and close your left and right nostrils.*
2. *First, breathe in one nostril (closing the second nostril) for a count of seven.*
3. *Hold (close both nostrils) for a count of four.*
4. *Now breathe out the second nostril (closing the first) for a count of seven.*
5. *Now breathe in the second nostril for a count of seven.*
6. *Hold for a count of four.*
7. *Breathe out the first nostril for a count of seven.*
8. *Repeat – continue 3-5 minutes.*

Alternate nostril breathing II

A more gentle form of the alternate nostril breathing exercise, this is for those who are new to this practice and may not wish to begin with focusing on breathing and counting. It focuses simply on the breath and the touch to the third eye.

1. *Take a comfortable seat. Create a long spine and open heart by sitting tall and resting your shoulder blades on your back.*
2. *Place your left hand comfortably in your lap and place your right hand in front of your face.*
3. *With your right hand, bring your index finger and middle finger to rest between your eyebrows, lightly using them as an anchor.*
4. *Close your right nostril with your right thumb. Inhale through the left nostril slowly and steadily.*
5. *Close the left nostril with your ring finger so both nostrils are held closed. For a brief pause, retain your breath at the top of the inhale.*
6. *Open your right nostril and release the breath slowly and steadily through the right side. Briefly pause at the bottom of the exhale.*
7. *Inhale through the right side slowly and steadily.*
8. *Hold both nostrils closed (with ring finger and thumb).*
9. *Open your left nostril and release the breath slowly and steadily through the left side. Briefly pause at the bottom of the exhale.*

Note: Steps 4-9 is one complete cycle of alternate nostril breathing. One cycle might take thirty or forty seconds if you are moving through the sequence slowly and steadily.

Practice this method by moving through five cycles when you are feeling overwhelmed, or stressed and need to hit the reset button. Consistency helps. Try matching the length of inhales, pauses, and exhales. An example of this would be to start to inhale for a count of 3, hold for 3, exhale for three counts. You can increase your counts as your practice grows.

Equal Breathing

This is helpful for balancing the breath throughout the body. It is supportive for calming the nervous system and reducing stress. This form of breathing is done through the nose, which adds a slight amount of resistance.

1. *Take a comfortable seat. Create a long spine and open heart by sitting tall and resting your shoulder blades on your back.*
2. *Inhale for a count of four.*
3. *Exhale for a count of four. Increase the length of the inhales and exhales by adding in either or both of the following:*
   - ***Increase inhale/exhale to six or eight breaths.***
   - ***Add in Ocean Breathing (ujjayi breathing):***
     - *Close your mouth and begin breathing in and out through the nose only.*
     - *Inhale through your nose slightly deeper than your normal inhale.*
     - *Exhale slowly through your nose while constricting the muscles at the back of the throat.*
     - *This sound will be similar to waves of the ocean. Or if you are familiar with the movie Star Wars, it sounds like Darth Vader breathing!*
     - *Some people also equate the feeling to sipping air through a straw.*

PROGRESSIVE RELAXATION MEDITATION

Start in a comfortable sitting position. (Lying down for this exercise is not recommended unless you are trying to fall asleep.)

Close your eyes, sit up tall, and rest your shoulder blades on your back.

Begin breathing through the nose calmly and evenly into the belly.

Slowly roll both shoulders forward three times, then roll them backward three times.

Lower your left ear toward your left shoulder and hold for a count of ten.

Float the head back to an upright position and hold for a count of ten.

Lower your right ear toward your right shoulder and hold for a count of ten.

Float the head back to an upright position.

Mentally scan your body and check that your muscles are relaxed.

Continue to breathe calmly and evenly into the belly.

Gently note your breathing pattern and how your breath flows in and out.

Do not try to control your breathing; simply breathe in and out at your own pace.

When your attention wanders, gently bring it back to the breathing.

If stray thoughts cross your mind, don't dwell on them but let them float through your consciousness.

Continue to breathe calmly and evenly into the belly.

Feel the air entering your nose and your belly gently rise and fall with each breath.

Inhale and silently focus on a word (OM, one, peace, shanti, breathe, or a word of your choosing).

Exhale and silently focus on your word.

Inhale – word

Exhale – word

Inhale – word

Exhale – word

Mentally scan your body and notice how it feels.

Notice how calm and gentle your breathing is and how relaxed your body feels

Keeping your eyes closed, begin to reconnect with your space.

Notice the feel of the chair or floor under you.

Become aware of the sounds around you.

Continue to breathe through the nose and into the belly.

Wiggle your fingers and toes.
Slowly roll both shoulders forward three times, and then roll them backward
three times.
Slowly open your eyes.
When you are ready, stand and stretch, reaching for the ceiling.
Bend forward and reach for the floor.
Bend side to side, stretching your muscles.
Wrap your arms around you, giving yourself a hug.
Shrug your shoulders up and then down.
Release the hug and shake out your body.
Energized and calm, you can now return to your day.

WALKING MEDITATION

This can be a helpful way to develop mindfulness of your physical state while at the same time develop a connection between mind and body. Many people find this form of meditation to be very calming. There is something soothing about focusing on and being more aware of your physical presence when you are engaged in the gentle act of walking. Consider planning for fifteen to thirty minutes, depending on the amount of time you have available.

This form of meditation can be done indoors or outside. Some walking meditations involve the use of a labyrinth, but this is not necessary. Simply have a comfortable space where you can walk twenty to thirty paces back and forth or in a circular pattern.

Standing tall, connect with the physical sensations of your body, from your feet resting on the ground to how your body is balanced when simply standing.
Keep your hands by your sides and your head elevated above your shoulders.
Try to feel the environment around you, noting the temperature, any wind, or other sensations as they come to your attention.
Begin to walk, slowly and deliberately placing one foot in front of the other.
Note the sensations as you lift each foot up and swing it forward into position for the next step. Note any other physical sensations such as the movement of your arms.
Pay attention to your body. With each step feel the sensations of lifting your foot and leg off the earth, then note the sensations as you place your foot back down. Feel each step mindfully as you walk.
When you reach the end of your path or circuit, turn around (or continue on if it's a circle), being mindful of how your body feels.
Retaining an awareness of your body, begin to notice your breath in response to your movements.
If desired, change speeds, choosing to move more quickly, slower, or alternating speeds at different points.
If your mind wanders, note it and make a decision to pull yourself back into awareness of your walking and any affiliated sensations.
When you are done walking, stop for a moment and note all of your body sensations. The very act of walking is your focus.

METTA, OR LOVING-KINDNESS, MEDITATION

This is a wonderful form of meditation for helping to develop a sense of connectedness with others and with the world around us. Research shows positive benefits come out of this simple practice of thinking good wishes for others and the world around us.

A Metta meditation is broken down into five parts, each part spoken aloud or thought quietly but with focus and intention:

1. *Sit comfortably, take several centering breaths, and then start with self-love by directing a statement toward yourself.*
2. *Next repeat the statement but visualize and direct it toward someone you care about.*
3. *Then repeat the statement, visualizing and directing it toward someone whom you are not connected to either positively or negatively.*
4. *Next, visualize and direct the statement to someone you struggle with.*
5. *Finally, direct the statement to the entire world.*

An example might look something like this:

Directed toward yourself:
May I be nurtured and nourished
Directed toward someone you care about:
May you be nurtured and nourished
Directed toward someone you dislike or struggle with:
May you be nurtured and nourished
Directed toward your family or community:
May we be nurtured and nourished
Directed to all sentient beings in the world:
May we all be nurtured and nourished

*The path of mindfulness and reflection
leads to inner wisdom*

AUTHOR BIOGRAPHIES

KERRY MCCLURE, BS, RYT, NC, BCHN®

Kerry is a health and wellness practitioner of nutrition, yoga, meditation, mindfulness, and fitness and creator of *"The Vibrant Life Method"* online wellness course. Kerry works with people to eat, move, and practice mindfulness for better energy; a clear, focused mind; and a long, healthy life free from chronic symptoms of illness.

Kerry is passionate about helping her clients shift their lifestyle from "surviving" to "thriving" and from feeling "normal" to feeling "optimal". She is known for delivering uplifting experiences and motivation through speaking engagements, private and group consulting, teaching movement classes and workshops, and leading online educational courses and webinars.

Kerry is Board Certified Holistic Nutrition®. She is a member of the National Association of Nutrition Professionals and The Yoga Alliance. She is certified in yoga, and several fitness modalities. She brings 25+ years of experience in corporate America to her company, Kerry McClure – Practical Wellness.

Learn more at www.KerryMcClure.com.

MIRA DESSY, BFA, NE, BCHHP

Mira Dessy is known as The Ingredient Guru, she teaches how to navigate the grocery store's mammoth packaged food stock, to decipher confusing food labels, understand the relationship of food additives to poor health, and to find real food. A holistic nutritionist and a popular public speaker, she knows that it's not just what you eat, but what's in what you eat. She is the author of the book *The Pantry Principle: how to read the label and understand what's really in your food.*

Mira is a member of the National Association of Nutrition Professionals, the Society for Nutrition Education and Behavior, the American Association of Drugless Practitioners, and the American Holistic Health Association. She has been working with clients for over 10 years, supporting them in reaching their health goals through holistic nutrition, lifestyle modifications, and chemical cleanup. Her motto is "Eat well to be well."

Mira can be found online at www.TheIngredientGuru.com.

FRIEND AND COLLEAGUE
BIOGRAPHIES

AJAYAN BORYS is author of *Effortless Mind: Meditate with Ease.* He offers video instruction and guided meditations on his meditation membership site at *www.Ajayan.com.*

—⁘∞∞∞∞⁘—

DR. ARLAND HILL, DC, MPH, DACBN, is a functional nutrition doctor who places great emphasis on food and how the connection we have to it influences our health. He is also an author and founder of Food, Function, Freedom, a resource that provides individuals with a five-step process to regain their health. His core belief is that optimal health is a choice that begins with reconnecting to food.

—⁘∞∞∞∞⁘—

BEDROS KEUILIAN is a highly sought-after peak performance coach. He's the guy that authors, experts, and entrepreneurs turn to when they want to multiply their success by ten times in half the time. He can be found online at *www.BedrosKeuilian.com.*

—⁘∞∞∞∞⁘—

CORY ROSS, with her Canadian farm background and international work and travel experience, lives in Ashland Oregon. She had a career as a management consultant before becoming an artist painting life experience: spiritual development, beauty, nature, and sometimes politics.

DON MCCLURE is a retired IT professional who is enthusiastic about the possibilities of a world without war and strife. It is possible and inevitable! So let's do it sooner!

—⚬⚬⚬⚬⚬—

ERIN KNIGHT, with her four-step Migraine Freedom plan, helps professional women suffering from chronic migraine experience a dramatic increase in productivity and start participating in life again. *www.EngineeringRadiance.com*

—⚬⚬⚬⚬⚬—

HALLIE MOORE's life has been anchored by meditation for three decades; she has been inspiring meditators for more than twenty years. A serious student of Eknath Easwaran, founder of the Blue Mountain Center of Meditation, she coordinates a weekly passage meditation group near Houston. Growing up on the West Coast, she attended Stanford University, B.A, M.A., Phi Beta Kappa, and Antioch University Los Angeles, MFA. She is an award winning poet and essayist who teaches creative writing and leads workshops. She can be found online at *www.HallieMoore.com*.

—⚬⚬⚬⚬⚬—

DR. HELAYNE WALDMAN, ED.D., is a board certified holistic nutrition professional who specializes in working with cancer patients through all phases of their cancer journey. She is the co-author of the Amazon bestselling book, *The Whole Food Guide for Breast Cancer Survivors*, and blogs for premier health sites such as GreenMedInfo and JoanLunden.com. Dr. Waldman is on the nutrition faculty of Hawthorn University and the Functional Medicine Program at the University of Western States. She also lectures regularly at conferences and organizations such as Annie Appleseed, The Cancer Control Society, The Wellness Community, Breast Cancer Connections, Sutter Medical Center, Women's Cancer Resource Center and the National Association of Nutrition Professionals. With her associate, Dr. Shani Fox, Dr. Waldman founded and co-facilitates the first live, online, interactive program for cancer survivors in the U.S.: Renew! Expert Care and Coaching for Cancer Survivors.

— ∞∞∞∞ —

JONAH DAS is a Kripalu-certified yoga teacher and musician. He teaches and practices in Kripalu and Bhakti yoga and has been leading kirtans, meditation gatherings, and prayer services in yoga studios, synagogues, and churches since 2006. He lives in Half Moon Bay, California, and Portland, Oregon.

— ∞∞∞∞ —

DR. KEESHA EWERS is board certified in functional medicine and Ayurvedic medicine, as well as being a doctor of sexology, psychotherapist, energy worker, yoga teacher, and founder and a host of the Healthy YOU! Radio network (*www.HealthyYouRadio.com*). She is the founder of a field of medicine called Functional Sexology, and through the Academy for Integrative Medicine, she offers a certification course for those passionate about and wanting to become Integrative Medicine health coaches. Her online programs and videos can be found at *www.DrKeesha.com*.

— ∞∞∞∞ —

KIRSTIN NUSSGRUBER, C.N.C., EMB, is a certified holistic nutritional consultant and health coach. She is an empathetic cancer mentor, speaker, and educator who is passionate about enabling women with breast cancer to pro-actively navigate their health challenge to achieve a conscious sense of accomplishment and balanced perspective. Her approach incorporates five key areas of health: functional nutrition, reducing toxicity, exercise, conscious living, and emotional healing.

After being diagnosed with breast cancer twice within three years, she learned first-hand the importance of an integrative and functional medicine approach to one's health, acknowledging the dynamic interdependence of body, mind, and soul to facilitate true healing.

Kirstin offers individualized 1-on-1 mentoring, can be hired for inspirational speaking engagements, and produces virtual interactive programs such as the Beyond Cancer Program™. For more information visit Kirstin's website at ***www.KirstinsCancerCare.com.***

—◈◈◈—

KYRIN DUNSTON MD, the author of *Cracking the Bikini Code: 6 Secrets to Permanent Weight Loss Success*, specializes in natural women's health care and weight loss. She prescribes meditation to all of her patients as part of their healing program, because it provides gifts that no pill can deliver.

—◈◈◈—

MARCIA SIVEK is a nutritionist in Los Gatos, CA. She has an MS in nutrition from the University of Bridgeport Connecticut. She sees a number of clients online and teaches various nutrition classes online and in person to those experiencing chronic conditions such as type 2 diabetes, autoimmune diseases, cancer, and those who want to age gracefully.

—◈◈◈—

MARGARET FLOYD is a nutritional therapist, writer, and real food advocate. She's the author of *Eat Naked: Unprocessed, Unpolluted and Undressed Eating for a Healthier, Sexier You* and co-author of *The Naked Foods Cookbook: The Whole Foods, Healthy Fats, Gluten-free Guide to Losing Weight and Feeling Great*. Margaret has an extensive private practice specializing in clients with stubborn chronic illness. She teaches advanced functional nutrition with Restorative Wellness Solutions ***www.RestorativeWellnessSolutions.com*** and blogs at ***www.EatNakedNow.com***.

MELISSA CRISPELL, CNS, CNHP, is a clinical nutritionist, a certified natural healthcare practitioner, a certified wellness coach, the owner of Long Term Wellness, a friend of First State Health & Wellness, and a nationally recognized functional nutrition speaker. She has over ten years experience helping clients understand the connection between pH balance, food and chemical sensitivities, physical fitness, and their overall health goals.

MELISSA HUMPHRIES is a former beauty queen who tossed off her tiara and high heels to follow a lifelong passion for holistic health and wellness. She is certified in personal training, functional fitness, levels I, II and III Living Foods Chef, nutritional therapy, and Integrative Health Coaching. Melissa founded Queen Bee Wellness to specialize her professional practice towards women's wellness and beauty with the goal of helping women reclaim their radiant health by balancing mind, body, and soul. Melissa believes that what we put in our hearts and minds is as important as the nourishing food we put in our bodies and healthy products on our skin. She coaches women to balance a healthier body image, a mindful approach to wellness, and tips on living their most beautiful lives.

With her passion for a naturalist lifestyle, Melissa formulates Queen Bee Wellness therapeutic skin care products to help women enhance their natural glow without causing harm to their health from chemical-laden toxic products. Melissa teaches workshops, leads retreats, and offers one on one personal coaching. Learn more at *www.QueenBeeWellness.com.*

MICHAEL AND ROBIN MASTRO are considered authorities in helping their clients live more productive and stress-free lives through the Vedic sciences. They are award-winning authors, experts, and educators of Vastu Shastra, the ancient East Indian science of environmental balance and harmony. Vastu eliminates the stress in homes and workspaces for greater success and well-being in all areas of life. They work with individuals around the world and corporate clients such as Microsoft, Boeing, Amazon, NASA, The World Bank and Oracle.

Michael Mastro is a Vastu consultant, award-winning author, Vedic astrologer, and Ayurvedic practitioner.

Robin Mastro is an environmental designer and author of Vedic knowledge. For more information, please visit: *www.VastuCreations.com* or call 206-661-1117.

—◇◆◆◇—

PAUL REYNOLDS, in this go-'round, has taken on the roles of author, cartoonist, yogi, teacher, father, partner, and interviewer of "inspiration in the everyday" on Le Guru is You! Radio podcast series on iTunes. *www.LeGuruIsYou.com*

—◇◆◆◇—

RACHAEL PONTILLO is the bestselling author of the book *Love Your Skin, Love Yourself,* and co-author of *The Sauce Code*. She's an AADP and IAHC board certified International Health Coach, licensed aesthetician, and natural skincare formulator and educator. She's the president and co-founder of the Nutritional Aesthetics® Alliance, the creator of the popular skincare and healthy lifestyle blog and podcast, Holistically Haute™, as well as the 6-week online course, Create Your Skincare. She's an avid herbalist, self-professed skincare ingredient junkie, and lifelong learner. *www.RachaelPontillo.com*

SARICA CERNOHOUS is a licensed practitioner of acupuncture and Traditional Chinese Medicine. She is also the author of The Funky Kitchen and teaches on the importance and techniques of traditional food preparation. Visit her at *www.NaturallyLivingToday.com*.

—∞∞∞∞—

STACY MCCARTHY has worn many hats in her career in Silicon Valley, from a CPA to start-ups to a global director of strategic planning for a Fortune 10 organization. Now she is honored to coach current and future executives in bringing their whole selves to their work.

—∞∞∞∞—

DR. TANDY ELISALA inspires women to live their life with passion and purpose. She empowers women to love themselves first and lead a life that matters. She is a four-time #1 international bestselling author, Huff Post contributor, and Certified Success Coach. Learn more about Tandy at *www.TandyElisala.com/freegifts*.

You are a bright light in the universe

ACKNOWLEDGEMENTS

KERRY MCCLURE

I would like to acknowledge all the teachers, lineages, friends, acquaintances, and students who have crossed the path of my life. You have helped, and continue to help, me understand, learn, practice and share mindfulness and meditation. I offer a deep and grateful thank you for being my teachers in this life's journey.

Thanks and appreciation to Donna Mosher, who edited this book with wonderful grace and skill.

I would like to express my deep gratitude to my husband, Don, for his unwavering patience, guidance, love, support, enthusiastic encouragement, and useful critiques of this book.

Last and not least: I'd like to thank Mira Dessy for her kindness, compassion, creativity, insights, and willingness to co-write this book. I bow in gratitude.

MIRA DESSY

Writing a book is often a solitary practice. Yet it cannot be done alone. I am deeply grateful for each of the many teachers, friends, family, and clients in my life who motivate me to do the things I do. Your continued support and encouragement lead to the amazing feat of creating this book.

I would like to take a moment to acknowledge a just few of the many without whom this book would not have come into being.

First and always my loving husband, Steve, who is encouraging and supportive even when he doesn't understand what I'm doing.

For Donna Mosher, who has become more than an editor and is a valued and trusted friend.

And grateful, heartfelt thanks for my co-author Kerry without whom this book would not have been born. Working with you has been a joy and a delight. I love our synchronicity.

Made in the USA
San Bernardino, CA
11 August 2017